CHRISTIAN, DISCIPLE, OR SLAVE?

by Torben Søndergaard

CHRISTIAN, DISCIPLE, OR SLAVE?

Torben Søndergaard

CHRISTIAN, DISCIPLE, OR SLAVE?

By Torben Søndergaard

Copyright © 2014 by Torben Søndergaard

All rights reserved. This book is protected under the copyright laws of the United States of America. This book may not be copied or reprinted for commercial gain or profit. The use of short quotations or occasional page copying for personal or group study is permitted and encouraged. Permission will be granted on request.

Paperback: ISBN: 978-1-938526-65-7

epub (iBooks, Nook): ISBN: 978-1-938526-66-4

Mobi (Kindle): ISBN: 978-1-938526-67-1

eBook: ISBN: 978-1-938526-68-8

Published by LAURUS BOOKS

LAURUS BOOKS
P. O. Box 894
Locust Grove, GA 30248 USA
www.TheLaurusCompany.com

This book is also available in formats for electronic readers from their respective stores and in the Dutch language from Amazon.

TABLE OF CONTENTS

PREFACE 7

1. A THOUGHT EXPERIMENT 9

2. EXAMINE YOURSELVES 13

3. CONFESS JESUS AS LORD 17

4. THE CHRISTIANS AS THEY USED TO BE 21

5. A DISCIPLE OF JESUS 27

6. A SLAVE OF CHRIST 33

7. NOT IN OUR OWN WAY 39

8. MANY "CHRISTIANS," FEW DISCIPLES 43

9. TO OBEY JESUS 45

10. WHAT A FANTASTIC LORD 49

11. BAPTIZED TO BELONG TO CHRIST 53

12. BAPTISM IN THE HOLY SPIRIT 57

13. REVELATION AND LIFE 63

14. HONORING GOD – YOUR SPIRITUAL SERVICE 69

15. LET NOT MY WILL BUT YOURS BE DONE 75

16. THE PRICE OF PEING A CHRISTIAN 79

17. PERSECUTION AND TRIBULATION 83

18. FRIENDS OF JESUS AND CHILDREN OF GOD 87

19. CONCLUSION 91

ABOUT THE AUTHOR 99

PREFACE

My great wish for this book is to create a debate about the meaning of being a Christian—a debate that is needed both inside and outside of the church.

Many people in the church live in a state of deceit that has taken them far away from the Christianity we read about in the Bible, the Christianity which saves and transforms. These "Christians" are the product of a "Christianity" that in some ways is very distant from what the Bible says. If you are one of them, you are among many who need to hear the real Gospel and start to live the life God has for you, a strong life with Jesus Christ as your Lord and Savior, a life that many deceived Christians actually want and long for.

The average person who normally knows Christianity only through some church activities also needs to hear the real Gospel about salvation through faith in Jesus. They need the message in this book to show them that Christianity is much more than what they believed or thought about it.

Today, we see people converting to Islam because they feel that Christianity is so diluted. The other day, I heard an interview with a Dane who had just converted to Islam. The reason he gave was that, in Islam, you have some specific things to relate to, in contrast to Christianity where, in his understanding, you could live the way you wanted to as long as you went to church. Yes, it is clear that he does

7

not know the Christianity that Jesus came with and that is still practiced in many places all around the world. However, his statement shows the picture of Christianity the way many imagine it today; a misleading picture that is far away from the biblical description and the true Christian life practiced by millions of Christians all over the world: a strong personal and dedicated life with Jesus as Lord. I hope this book can help us do something about that.

You can help by starting this debate about what a Christian really is so that we can soon see a change in Europe, America, and around the world. You can also make a difference by spreading the message in this book, by beginning to use the words "disciple" and "slave" instead of the word "Christian," which has been so diluted. Just by beginning to use these words, we can throw a completely new light over Christianity and its purpose and take a step toward a change within the churches and outside of them.

Enjoy the read. My hope is that this book will make a change in your life as you see your place in the relationship with Jesus and His Word concerning following Him.

God bless you.

Torben Søndergaard
A disciple of Jesus Christ

CHAPTER ONE

A THOUGHT EXPERIMENT

Try to imagine there is not even one Christian in the whole world. You are not a Christian, and you have never heard about Christianity. There are no churches, no Christian books, no Christian TV, or Christian newspapers. There is nothing that directly has anything to do with Christianity.

One day you find a book titled *Holy Bible*. You have never before seen or heard about the Bible, Jesus, or Christianity. You start reading the Old Testament about how it all began and how the land of Israel came into existence. You read how God works with His people and see a clear picture of God as holy and righteous, a God who can become angry but who is also merciful and patient, a God who has great love for His people, a God who will one day send us all a Savior, which is the Red Thread throughout the Old Testament. When you get to the end of the Old Testament, you already have an impression of what God is like and how He acts. You continue by reading the New Testament. There, you begin to see the Savior whom God promised.

You read the four Gospels, which tell how Jesus Christ went around preaching the Gospel and healing the sick. Page after page, you read how He preached that people should repent and believe in the Gospel, that everyone who wants to inherit the Kingdom of God should take up their cross and follow Him. You read about all the other radical things He said and did. The Gospels tell you how He took disciples and then sent them out to preach the Gospel and heal the sick. You read that He was loved by some and hated by others. You read how He gave Himself on the cross for all of us and how, through His death and resurrection, He conquered death. Everything put together gives you a really good understanding of who Jesus was and what He preached.

After completing the Gospels, you continue by reading Acts, where you see that after His resurrection, Jesus came and said that those who believed in Him would receive power from above when the Holy Spirit came upon them. Then you read about how it actually happened. As you read through Acts, you start to understand how the first Christians lived. It was a life with a lot of opposition and persecution. It cost everything to follow Jesus. It was a supernatural life in fellowship with God and each other, a life where the Christians went around and preached the Gospel, with signs and wonders following.

After Acts, you move on to the Book of Romans. In the first four chapters, you read that we have all sinned and gone far away from God. You go to chapter five that describes Jesus as the new Adam who was supposed to forgive us and reconcile us with God. Chapters six through eight say that, in Christ, there is freedom from sin and that this freedom comes when you get baptized and walk in obedience to the Spirit instead of the flesh. After that, you come to chapters nine and ten, which explain that you get saved by making Jesus your Lord.

When you read this, you bow on your knees and ask Jesus to come and be your Lord and save you. Then you immediately experience the new birth the Bible talks about, salvation in Christ, and soon you get baptized in the Holy Spirit, which you have read about over and over again in Acts.

As you are there on your knees, born again, you can feel a difference inside. Now you know that you have been forgiven and that what the Bible says is true because you have experienced it in your body, and you have this testimony inside of you. You rise, determined to follow Jesus 100% and start by baptizing yourself in water because there is no one else to do it.

From that moment on, you begin to live as a Christian based on what you read in the *Holy Bible*, which is the only description of the Christian life you know. It is your only instruction book and the only place that can give you the answer when it comes to what God is like. You begin to use it as your mirror because there are no other Christians you can compare yourself with or ask how things work. The only thing you have is the Bible and the Holy Spirit to reveal it to you.

Ask yourself now: If it was you, how do you think you would live?

Do you think you would live as you do now?

Do you think you would live as most Christians do today?

Or, do you think you would discover something other than what we see in modern Christianity?

Do you think you would have another understanding of who God is and what it actually means to live as a Christian?

The truth is that if you started to believe in Jesus by reading His preaching, and if the *Holy Bible* was your only available resource, you would surely discover something other than what we see in many places today. First of all, Jesus preached very radically. Secondly, you would completely build your life on the Word and not like many do today with a little bit built on the Word and a little bit built on our "Christian" culture.

One of our biggest problems today is that we as Christians so quickly compare ourselves not to the Bible but to one another and to our Christian culture. We look at our fellow Christians and think: "If he can live like that and still be a Christian, then I can do that, too." We look at our churches and think: "If they conduct their services in this way, it must be right. They have been doing it for many years, so they must know what is best." And when we read the New Testament about the power and the life of the first Christians, we think: "Yes, it was something special at that time, but it is clearly another time today where things are different." This is, however, not only a wrong way to understand it, but it is also dangerous because we should build on the Word of God alone and not on our culture or what other Christians around us are doing. We must always follow God's way first.

As you are reading this book, try to ignore what the "Christian" culture says and how other Christians around you live. If you succeed in that and are open to what the Word of God says, this book can change your life and save you from perishing. In this book, I am trying to draw a picture of what it means to live as a Christian according to the *Holy Bible*, God's Word. Let us therefore compare ourselves to the Word of God instead of to one another and to our culture. Let us read what the Bible says and be changed into the same image we see there, from glory to glory.

> *But we all, with unveiled face, beholding as in a mirror the glory of the Lord, are being transformed into the same image from glory to glory, just as from the Lord, the Spirit.* (2 Corinthians 3:18 NAS)

CHAPTER TWO

EXAMINE YOURSELVES

Some of the content of this book will sound very radical and strange to many. The reason is that we have slowly moved so far away from the Christianity we read about in the Bible. We live in a time when people gather teachers to themselves according to their own lusts instead of listening to what the Bible really says.

> *For the time will come when men will not put up with sound doctrine. Instead, to suit their own desires, they will gather around them a great number of teachers to say what their itching ears want to hear.* (2 Timothy 4:3 NIV)

They say that "truth hurts," and it is sometimes true. We have to remember, however, that even if the truth hurts, it is still the truth, and the truth will set us free, as Jesus says. Christianity has changed a lot in comparison to the first church that we read about in the Bible. Even in the last decades, it has experienced big changes, especially in the western world. One of the things that looks different is the preaching, and especially our relation to faith. Today, you can hear in many places that we as Christians should not ask ourselves whether our faith is good enough. This is exactly the opposite of what the Bible says and of what Christians used to say a few decades ago.

> *Put yourselves to the test and judge yourselves, to find out whether you are living in faith. Surely you know that Christ Jesus is in you?*

Unless you have completely failed. (2 Corinthians 13:5 GNT)

Here, we can read that Paul challenges us to examine our faith. It does not mean that we should question our faith every single minute, but Paul says that we as Christians should prove ourselves and see if we are really in the faith. We have to examine ourselves because if Christ is not in us, we will fail the test. We have to read what the Word says about faith and living with Christ and then see if it is compatible with our life. If it is not, we have to repent and come to faith. This is important if we are supposed to pass the test.

Examining and repenting is something that we as Christians have to do over and over again because we learn something new all the time. God is constantly working in us and wants us to be closer to Him. That is why, as a Christian, you must never sit back and think that you have grasped it. No, instead, you have to ask yourself:

How do I live in comparison to the Bible?

Is Christ really in me, or am I still living in conscious sin?

Have I walked away from a pure and sincere relationship with Jesus? Have I ever been there?

It is especially important to do this because we are all influenced by the time and culture in which we are living. We live in a time when the Gospel is seldom preached in the pure and radical form that Jesus and the apostles preached. It is not always sound doctrine that is preached but, rather, something that tickles the ears, as we have read before. Therefore, we are all somehow influenced by the Christianity of today, which in many ways is not compatible with the Bible.

We have to examine ourselves by comparing ourselves to the Bible and not to our neighbors or the Christians in the church. If we do the latter, everything will go wrong. In some cases, it can end with a blind person leading another blind peson:

"Let them alone; they are blind guides of the blind. And if a blind man guides a blind man, both will fall into a pit." (Matthew 15:14 NAS)

Many preachers today, contrary to the preachers just a few decades ago, consider it their task to help the believers not to doubt their faith. At that time, the task of many preachers was to preach the Word as clearly as possible and thereby reveal if something was incompatible with the Bible. It created doubt in some people, and then the preacher's task was done. It showed that something was wrong, which hopefully made the person repent and experience forgiveness. This is clearly much better than continuing to live in deceit without Christ and failing your test one day.

Therefore, if this book strikes you and makes you see something from the Word that is wrong in your life, be thankful and do something about it. It is better to see it now than to experience that terrible day when you stand before Jesus and hear Him say: "Away from me, I do not know you who commit sin."

Today, you can find forgiveness and salvation.

CHAPTER THREE

CONFESS JESUS AS LORD

We begin this chapter by looking at some of the things Jesus says about salvation and confessing Him as Lord.

"Enter through the narrow gate; for the gate is wide and the way is broad that leads to destruction, and there are many who enter through it. For the gate is small and the way is narrow that leads to life, and there are few who find it." (Matthew 7:13-14 NAS)

After this eye-opener, Jesus goes on to talk about how we can get to know people by their fruit, or their deeds, and He continues the warning with these frightening words:

"Not everyone who says to Me, 'Lord, Lord,' will enter the kingdom of heaven, but he who does the will of My Father who is in heaven will enter. Many will say to Me on that day, 'Lord, Lord, did we not prophesy in Your name, and in Your name cast out demons, and in Your name perform many miracles?' And then I will declare to them, 'I never knew you; DEPART FROM ME, YOU WHO PRACTICE LAWLESSNESS.'" (Matthew 7:21-23 NAS)

As we can understand from these verses, very few of all those who call Jesus "Lord" will get to heaven. He is saying that the gate is narrow and the way is narrow, or constricted, and that only a few find it. He is also saying that, one day, He will tell many who confess Him as Lord:

17

"I have never known you. Away from me, you who break the law!" It is therefore not enough to say, "Lord, Lord," to Jesus and believe that everything is all right, like many do today.

When you have the word "Lord" used twice, it is because of the way authors expressed themselves in the texts from those times. If we want to emphasize something today, we write it with BLOCK LETTERS, in italics, or in bold. They did not do it that way in the past; they repeated themselves instead. Therefore, when it says, "Lord, Lord," it does not really mean that the person repeats the word twice. The person says "LORD" once, but from the heart and with emphasis. When Jesus says that not all who say "Lord, Lord" to Him will go to heaven, He is not thinking about those who stand with their hands in their pockets, chewing gum, while they half-heartedly mumble: "Jesus is my Lord." No, the words of Jesus are even more serious: He is talking about the people who call Him "LORD" and really mean it, at least in their own way and out of their own understanding.

Terrifying words, are they not? Nevertheless, they are the words of Jesus, and this fact must make anyone who is a Christians stop and evaluate their life according to Jesus' words and to the rest of the Bible.

In Luke chapter six, Jesus says:

"Why do you call Me, 'Lord, Lord,' and do not do what I say?" (Luke 6:46 NAS)

This is a good question to ask. Why do you call Him "Lord" if you do not mean it, or if you do not act like what He says?

After His question, Jesus continues to tell a parable about building on a rock and not on the sand.

"Everyone who comes to Me and hears My words and acts on them, I will show you whom he is like: he is like a man building a house, who dug deep and laid a foundation on the rock; and when a flood occurred, the torrent burst against that house and could not shake it, because it had been well built. But the one who has heard and has not acted accordingly, is like a man who built a house on the ground without any foundation; and the torrent burst against it and immediately it collapsed, and the ruin of that house was great." (Luke 6:47-49)

It is clear from this parable that the difference between those who build on the ground, or sand, and those who build on the rock is whether you do what He says or not. Again, it has not so much to do with the confession but with how you live. We can easily confess Jesus as Lord with our mouth without making Him Lord in our heart and living accordingly.

When you talk about obedience, many might say that you are talking about deeds and that Christianity is not a religion of deeds. Of course, I want to say that you cannot get saved through your deeds, but only through faith in Jesus. True faith will, however, result in obedience to Him because we believe that what He says is right, and that is why we live accordingly with full confidence. Then the deeds will always be a natural part of the faith.

"For just as the body without the spirit is dead, so also faith without works is dead." (James 2:26 NAS)

Naturally, it has nothing to do with a lot of achievements, but with Jesus and our inner life, which will also become clear farther on in this book. It is not about deeds for the deeds' sake, but about the life with Him, a life that quite naturally produces deeds.

If you ask Christians today how to get saved, many will surely say that it happens through believing and confessing Jesus as Lord. Is that not what the well-known verse in Romans chapter ten says?

"If you declare with your mouth, "Jesus is Lord," and believe in your heart that God raised him from the dead, you will be saved." (Romans 10:9 NIV)

Yes, this is true. The point I want to make here, however, is that even though it seems to be so clear here, many will one day say, "Lord, Lord," to Him, but they will not get into heaven. When Jesus Himself asks why you call Him "Lord, Lord" when you do not act according to His Word, it is because the confession in itself does not save. What saves you is what lies behind the confession and gives you the reason for confessing, "Jesus is my Lord."

In Matthew chapter 21, Jesus gives the parable about the two sons in the vineyard. Try to give attention to the fact that the sons are not compared according to what they say but what they do.

"But what do you think? A man had two sons; and he came to the first and said, 'Son, go work in my vineyard.' And he answered, 'I will not'; but afterward he regretted it and went. The man came to the second and said the same thing; and he answered, 'I will, sir'; but he did not go. Which of the two did the will of his father?" They said, "The first." Jesus said to them, "Truly I say to you that the tax collectors and prostitutes will get into the kingdom of God before you. For John came to you in the way of righteousness and you did not believe him; but the tax collectors and prostitutes did believe him; and you, seeing this, *did not even feel remorse afterward so as to believe him." (Matthew 21:28-32 NASB)*

Therefore, not everyone who confesses Jesus as Lord will get into heaven, but only those who have Him as Lord, those who do God's will, as we have just read in the Gospel of Matthew.

It should be obvious and unnecessary to mention, but, unfortunately, that is not the case. Today's attitude toward faith and confession is that you can believe and confess one thing and do another. This has never been the purpose of the faith the Bible is talking about.

In the next chapters, it is going to become even more clear what true faith and Christianity is. It is going to be a discovery trip through the Word of God that is guaranteed to be exciting and, perhaps, also terrifying. It is exciting because the Word of God is the truth, and it is the truth that gives life and sets us free. If there is anything we need today, it is truth. It will be terrifying because the darkness and deceit will become visible when the Word of God casts light upon things. In this teaching, we want to let the Word of God show us how things really are. We will see how truly far away from God we have come and how wrong teaching has misled many Christians who think they are walking the narrow path.

That is why it is so important to examine ourselves over and over again to see if Christ really is in us, especially in these last days in which the Bible says that people will fall away from the true faith because of wrong teaching. This wrong teaching is described as "deceiving spirits and doctrines of demons" (1 Timothy 4:1).

CHAPTER FOUR

THE CHRISTIANS AS THEY USED TO BE

What does it mean to be a Christian? If we look at Christians today and compare ourselves with what we read in the New Testament, we will quickly see that we are missing something that the first Christians used to have. The Christianity we have today is much different from what we read about in the Bible.

For example, we do not have the boldness that the early disciples had. They could not stop talking about everything they had seen and done (Acts 4:20). Today, we do not see the signs and wonders that the first Christians did. In the Bible, we read that people literally took Paul's belt and laid it on the sick, so that they were healed, and the evil spirits went out (Acts 19:11). We read that Peter experienced the same things when just his shadow fell on the sick. They were healed, and the evil spirits left them (Acts 5:15). In many other ways, we can see a difference between those times and today.

I am one of those who believes in a revival and seeing people turning to God. I do not believe, however, that we are missing something new that the world has never seen before. I do not believe we need a new kind of Christianity, but a return to the old one. We need to come back to the beginnings of Christianity that we read about in the Bible. We have to return to God's intention and see how God comes near and works among us, as we can see on all the pages in Acts. In the Bible, we can see that God really worked strongly among them and daily added new people who got saved (Acts 2:47). We can read about the kind of love they had, both for God and for one another (1 John 4:20). It was the love that covers many sins and makes one willing to lay down their life for one another (John 15:13).

Yes, many things have changed.

I am convinced that one of the reasons we are not seeing the same things happening today is our lack of understanding of what it actually means to live with Jesus as Lord. Many Christians never really reach the point where it becomes a serious relationship where God is part of our daily life, where we see the continuation of the Acts, where it is us who serve Him, so that His will may be done. Most people see Him as the One who fulfills our will.

I believe one of the reasons for this misunderstanding—or this *deceit* because that is what it really is—is that we do not know the different words and expressions used in the Bible, such as "Lord," "Christian," or "disciple." We have given these words a different meaning, and that is why we can never reach the place where God wants us to be, the point where He can seriously work in our dead flesh as He did in the first church.

When we talk about the cross, the most central point of Christianity, we talk about death. Jesus died on the cross in order to take our punishment. The choice that all people have to make today relates to the cross. Either we literally die on the cross and take our own punishment when it comes, or we die by the cross through making Jesus our Lord and no longer live for ourselves but for the One who died and rose again. You cannot deny the cross, even though many would like to. Dying to your own self is one of the keys to the life we read about in the Bible, and the key by itself.

There can be no doubt that the Christians in the apostles' time lived differently from how we live today, even though God is the same today as He was at that time. It is, therefore, not God nor Christianity that has changed; it is our lifestyle. When people look for new definitions for Christianity, you must be on alert. It is not new definitions that we need. What we are missing is a new demonstration. When we look deep into the Word of God, we will soon see where we have made a mistake.

What is a Christian?

The first word we will take a look at is "Christian." It is one of the words that is often misunderstood. Many people have misinterpreted it, which causes a lot of misunderstanding. Eventually, this creates a deception that makes many believe they are where they are not. Many who believe they are walking on the narrow path are actually walking on the broad one, the road to perdition.

Many Christians cannot understand why modern Christianity is so different from the Bible. In many places, they are served evasive explanations about today being a different time and God working in another way. The answer, however, is somewhere else.

One of the most important reasons is that many people misunderstand the word "Christian," and therefore they also misunderstand what it means to be a Christian. That is why they have no life, power, or love. What is even worse, it also means that many will perish forever if nothing happens. Many people consider themselves Christians due to wrong understanding of the Word. When they hear that Christians go to heaven, they think it is valid for them. Many, however, build on something that will not stand on the day the truth comes. It is very important that we do not misunderstand the real meaning of this word "Christian." Let us then go back to the place where the word "Christian" first appeared and see what lies behind it.

If you look for the word "Christian" or "Christians" in a biblical lexicon, you will see that it is found only three times in the whole Bible. The first time it appears is around the year 44 AD, eleven years after Jesus walked upon the earth and after the birth of the church.

> ... and the disciples were first called Christians in Antioch. (Acts 11:26 NAS)

You may have heard someone teach that "being a Christian" and "being a disciple of Jesus" are two different things. It is a thought shared by many, even though they do not talk about it so much.

Such an understanding implies that you become a Christian by believing in Jesus and then you go to heaven when you die. After you have already become a Christian, you can take a step further and become a disciple of Jesus if you want to, but it is completely voluntary.

Jesus' tough requirement of denying yourself if you want to be a disciple makes many choose to be just "Christians." Living as a disciple requires, namely, that you are fully devoted in all areas of life, which we are going to take a look at later.

The truth is, however, that you cannot differentiate between "being a Christian" and "being a disciple" because they are the same thing. You cannot be a Christian without being a disciple.

We are clearly reading in this verse that it was the disciples who were called "Christians,: so already we have to exclude the possibility of two different groups. If it was right that you first became a Christian by believing in Jesus and then you could choose to become a disciple, then the verse is wrong. It would have to say that it was in Antioch that the Christians were first called disciples, and not that disciples were called Christians, as it actually says. You cannot, therefore, differentiate between the two.

Those three thousand people who came to faith at Pentecost when the apostle Peter was preaching did not just become believers, or Christians, as many people today interpret these notions. They all became disciples of Jesus.

The word "Christian" did not exist at all at that time. It was first introduced eleven years later as a sort of nickname given to the disciples by the heathens. It came from the word "Christ," or the Anointed One. They were called Christians because, in many ways, they resembled Christ in their lifestyles. They were His followers. However, the word that was used by the disciples and Jesus Himself was "disciple"—a disciple of Jesus.

As it has been said, the word "Christian" or "Christians" can be found only three times in the whole Bible, and the first time we come across it is eleven years after the first church was started.

The word "disciple," however, is used more than 200 times just in the New Testament, and it was the word used by everyone, including Jesus when He gave the great commission to His disciples. It is important to remember that, at that time, neither He nor the rest of the world knew the word "Christian."

And Jesus came and spoke to them, saying, "All authority is given to Me in heaven and on earth. Go therefore and make disciples of all the nations, baptizing them in the name of the Father and of the Son and of the Holy Spirit, teaching them to observe all things that I have commanded you; and lo, I am with you always, even to the end of the age" (Matthew 28:18-20 NKJV)

The commission given by Jesus was that we should make disciples of all people, baptizing them in the name of the Father, the Son, and the Holy Spirit, and by teaching them to observe everything He has commanded. It is still the same today.

Do not let anyone deceive you into believing that a Christian and a disciple are two different things. You cannot be a Christian and get saved without being a disciple of Jesus with all its implications.

CHAPTER FIVE

A DISCIPLE OF JESUS

The word "disciple," just like the word "Christian," is often misunderstood because it is not used in our culture. In the Bible, you can read that many had their own disciples. For example, John the Baptist and Moses. In those days, disciples were a natural part of daily life. One of the first times we find the word used in connection with Jesus is in the Gospel of Matthew, chapter 4, where Jesus gave this name to His first disciples.

In E-SWORD, an electronic version of the Bible, one of the commentaries says:

> "They must separate themselves to a diligent attendance on him, and set themselves to a humble imitation of him; must follow him as their Leader."

Therefore, in chapter four of the Gospel of Matthew when Jesus called His first disciples, He called them to put everything aside in order to follow Him. They were supposed to become His apprentices, follow Him, and learn from Him by watching His life. That is why a metaphor of being a disciple is "apprentice," or "student."

"The disciple is not above his master, but everyone who is perfect shall be like his master." (Luke 6:40)

The disciples of Jesus were his apprentices. Jesus was their master, and they followed him. The term "apprentice" was often used in our culture many years ago, but it is not so common nowadays. The big difference between apprenticeship and ordinary studies is that, in apprenticeship, you do not have the same school course as in an ordinary study course.

In apprenticeship, rather than sitting at a school bench, you learn by following and imitating your master's example, which is what we read about Jesus and His disciples. In Jesus' time, the requirements were much higher, however, than following your master eight hours a day and then having time off to do whatever you liked. You cannot make a close comparison here.

In order to comprehend the intended meaning of the word "disciple," the context the author had in mind must be understood. To say that the gospels were written in another time and culture and are completely different today is not a good reason to use our modern definition. We have to learn about the Author and the culture of His times in order to understand what it means when Jesus says that we should make people into His disciples.

Another difference about that time was respect for authorities. If we consider the respect shown to parents, the police, and school teachers, we will clearly see that it cannot be found among the youth of today, even in comparison to life just 20 years ago. A common trait of our modern culture is that we want to decide for ourselves what is right and wrong and not leave that to teachers and law enforcement. Unfortunately, to a large extent we can also observe this lack of respect with regard to people's relationship with Jesus. "He is not going to decide; I want to do it myself; it is my life; etc."

However, when Jesus said that we should go and make people into His disciples, He meant that everyone who wants to be His disciple has to put their own life aside in order to follow Him and learn from Him, to listen to Him and obey what He says.

The original understanding of discipleship is clearly expressed in the gospels, where we see how the disciples were with Jesus all the time. They learned from Him and did what He said to them, or at least tried to do it; they were far from perfection. On the day of Pentecost, the Holy Spirit came upon them and would help them to obey.

Up to this point, we have seen that the word "Christian" is something that was introduced as a nickname and was not used at the beginning or in the first church. Neither Jesus nor the first disciples used that word. It appears only three times in the whole Bible, while we see that the word "disciple" can be found more than 200 times in the New Testament alone.

We have seen that Jesus charged us to go and make people into His disciples. It happens by getting baptized into Him, as well as by following Him and learning to obey His commands. In other words, everybody has to become an apprentice of Jesus and live a life of following Him closely.

Therefore, it is important to understand the terms correctly to prevent confusion about God's purpose for us.

Here are some statements using the term "Christian" that I have heard many times:

- I am a Christian, but just in my own way.
- I am a Christian, but I am not so much involved in it.
- I am a Christian because I have been baptized and confirmed.
- I am a Christian, but I do not believe in the Bible.
- I am a Christian, but I do not believe in all this stuff with Jesus as the Son of God.

Now, let's use the correct word, which is "disciple." Read the same statements while considering what you have just learned about true discipleship.

- I am a disciple of Jesus, but just in my own way.
- I am a disciple of Jesus, but I am not so much involved in it.
- I am a disciple of Jesus because I have been baptized and confirmed.
- I am a disciple of Jesus, but I do not believe in the Bible.
- I am a disciple of Jesus, but I do not believe in all this stuff with Jesus as the Son of God.

I hope you are starting to understand the deception involved when it comes to the word "Christian." This is something very serious and shows how far we have strayed from original Christianity and sound doctrine. It is clear that these statements, made by so many people today, do not make sense. Many Christians have a totally wrong understanding of living with God, which shows that Jesus is not their Lord and Savior.

It is shocking to think that so many people nowadays have absolutely no problem saying the things we just read. They do not see the conflict. The deception does not only lie in the misunderstanding of the word "Christian," but also of what it means in biblical terms to live with Jesus. It has nothing to do with using nice words but with how we live and what we believe. Many people live in a deception and are going to be lost one day if they do not experience inner repentance.

Salvation does not imply adopting a nickname, which the word "Christian" really is. It is about being a disciple of Jesus. Not my disciple, not a priest's disciple, but a disciple of Jesus.

We are, first of all, disciples of Jesus. If we move the emphasis from Jesus to our leaders and human role models, it can be abused with the purpose of gaining power over others, which unfortunately has happened in some places. However, it is Jesus who has the power, and it is all about Jesus, even though He uses leaders to show us the way. That is why what matters ultimately is what He says to us today through His Word, the Bible. It is about seeking Him and letting the Holy Spirit reveal Him as He is and what He is saying to us.

Jesus says many things about being His disciples. One of the proofs is that we abide in His Word, which helps to prevent us from being deceived.

> "Then Jesus said to those Jews who believed Him, "If you abide in My word, you are My disciples indeed. And you shall know the truth, and the truth shall make you free." They answered Him, "We are Abraham's descendants, and have never been in bondage to anyone. How can You say, 'You will be made free'?" (John 8:31-33 NKJV)

A disciple abides in the words of Jesus. He or she reads and studies the Bible and obeys what it says. It is not possible to be a disciple of Jesus without obeying His words. It is impossible to be a Christian—if we still use the most common notion—without believing in the Bible and living according to it. The Bible, the Word of God, is what we should get our *life* from. Through the Word, we get to know the truth, which will set us free. It is through the Word that we get to know Jesus as the Way, the Truth, and the Life.

There will be some people who say that living according to the Bible is fundamentalism, and this is correct. The word "fundamentalism" comes from "building on a foundation," which in this case is the Bible. All Christians should be fundamentalists. I know that this word has come to have some bad connotations today because many people associate it with legalism or even Islam and its fundamentalists, but it is not dangerous to build on a biblical foundation. On the contrary, Jesus makes it clear that if you build on the rock, it is not enough to know what the Word says; you also have to live accordingly.

The other requirements of being a disciple of Jesus can be found in many places in all the gospels. It is important, however, to remember what Jesus says:

"Come to Me, all you who labor and are heavy laden, and I will give you rest. Take My yoke upon you and learn from Me, for I am gentle and lowly in heart, and you shall find rest to your souls. For My yoke is easy and My burden is light. " (Matthew 11:28-30 NKJV)

We can quickly make a mistake and take a heavy yoke upon ourselves when we read the words of Jesus to us, but if our own self and ambitions are dead, obedience is not a problem. Then it is not a heavy yoke, but pure pleasure.

The hardest thing is not our having to obey our Lord but, rather, having to die to ourselves. This is what the struggle is about. At the same time, we find power to overcome this struggle in obeying Jesus. It is not something we can achieve in our own power. In Him, we can find everything we need, including the power to follow Him.

This can not be used as an excuse to avoid obeying Him, but as help to know that what we need in order to obey can be found in fellowship with Him. We will take a look at this later.

CHAPTER SIX

A SLAVE OF CHRIST

I n Ephesians 6, Paul is telling slaves how they should serve their earthly masters.

"Slaves, obey your earthly masters with fear and trembling, with a sincere heart, as you would Christ" (Ephesians 6:5 ESV)

Slaves should thus serve their earthly masters in the same way as they would serve Christ, which means they should do it with fear and trembling, and with a sincere heart.

But is it not a bit of a radical comparison? Serving Christ does not have so much to do with being a slave, does it?

The truth is that if you delve into the Bible in its original language, you will see that the same word translated here and in other places as "slave" is rendered as "servant" in other biblical contexts. Here, it really starts to get exciting.

The word that here in Ephesians is translated as "slave" is *doulos*. The context in which it is found makes it clear that "slave" is the correct rendering of the word. It is the same in Paul's letter to Titus, where again in one passage of the text he refers to the slaves.

"Slaves are to be submissive to their own masters in everything; they are to be well-pleasing, not argumentative." (Titus 2:9 ESV)

Although you can see in many places that this word is correctly translated as "slave," it is translated in many other places as "servant." We can find an example in one of the parables of Jesus in the Gospel of Matthew:

> *"For it will be like a man going on a journey, who called his servants and entrusted to them his property." (Matthew 25:14 ESV)*

Since the word "doulos" is used here, it could have been translated as "slaves" instead of "servants": A man called his slaves and turned his property over to them.

Another place where this word is translated as "servants" is the episode where Jesus washes the disciples' feet:

> *"Truly, truly, I say to you, a servant is not greater than his master, nor is a messenger greater than the one who sent him.." (John 13:16 ESV)*

Again, it could just as well have been rendered as: *A slave is not greater than his master.* It is the same word that Paul uses when he addresses the slaves in his letters.

There are more places in the Bible where the word "servant" could be replaced by "slave," which is not completely irrelevant because being a servant has a slightly different meaning than being a slave. We will discuss that more in depth.

Let us go back to the verse in Ephesians again. This time we will follow it with the next verse in order to see even more clearly how you can translate the same word in two different ways.

> *"Slaves [doulos], obey your earthly masters with fear and trembling, with a sincere heart, as you would Christ, not by the way of eye-service, as people-pleasers, but as servants [doulos] of Christ, doing the will of God from the heart, rendering service with a good will as to the Lord and not to man." (Ephesians 6:5-7 ESV)*

They have thus decided to translate the word as "slave" in one place and as "servant" in the other. It should actually be rendered in this way:

> *"Slaves, obey your earthly masters with fear and trembling, with a sincere heart, as you would Christ, not by the way of eye-service, as people-pleasers, but as slaves of Christ, doing the will of God from the heart, rendering service with a good will as to the Lord and not*

to man." (Ephesians 6:5-7 ESV)

Exciting, isn't it?

It means something completely different when you use the expression "slave of Christ" instead of "servant of Christ." The word "slave" probably creates different associations in your mind, but as you gradually think about the meaning, you might, just as I, find the thought more liberating than restrictive.

A slave does not have so many worries. He does not have to worry about the future or earning money. His only task is to do what the master says.

We can also live in faith that every month God provides the money. It is so liberating! Of course, it does not imply that we are supposed to sit back and do nothing. A slave does not do his own will but serves and does his master's will. To be a Christian means to be a disciple and follower of Christ, a slave of Christ, one who does what his master wants.

Paul understood this just like all his contemporaries. This is what it means to follow Jesus:

"He [Jesus] died for all, so that they who live might no longer live for themselves, but for Him who died and rose again on their behalf." (2 Corinthians 5:15 NAS)

"For if we live, we live for the Lord, or if we die, we die for the Lord; therefore whether we live or die, we are the Lord's. " (Romans 14:8 NAS)

If we start to use these strong words—"disciple" or "slave"—instead of the word "Christian," which is misused today, we will see things as they are, and the deceit in which many live will be revealed.

Jesus says to everyone who wants to follow Him:

"And He was saying to them all, 'If anyone wishes to come after Me, he must deny himself, and take up his cross daily and follow Me. For whoever wishes to save his life will lose it, but whoever loses his life for My sake, he is the one who will save it. For what is a man profited if he gains the whole world, and loses or forfeits himself?' " (Luke 9:23-25 NAS)

This was understood in the time of Jesus. Paul, Peter, John, and the other disciples lived in that. They understood that they now belonged to someone else. To them, baptism was the sign that they could not live for themselves any longer. They were baptized to belong to Christ.

The great thing about laying down our lives for Jesus as His slaves is that He will not call us slaves:

"No longer do I call you slaves, for the slave does not know what his master is doing; but I have called you friends, for all things that I have heard from My Father I have made known to you." (John 15:15 NAS)

I will come back to this later.

Right now, the most important thing is to understand that it is just as correct, if not more correct, to say that we are Christ's slaves instead of His servants. We are His slaves, and that means that He is our Lord and we are obedient to Him.

Look again at the expressions we so often hear today using the word "Christian." These will be followed by the same comments using the words "a slave of Christ" to see the difference.

- I am a Christian, but just in my own way.
- I am a Christian, but I am not so much involved in it.
- I am a Christian because I have been baptized and confirmed.
- I am a Christian, but I do not believe in the Bible.
- I am a Christian, but I do not believe in all this stuff with Jesus as the Son of God.

Now read this version.

- I am a slave of Christ, and I belong to Him, but just in my own way.
- I am a slave of Christ, and I belong to Him, but I am not so much involved in it.
- I am a slave of Christ and I belong to Him because I have been baptized and confirmed.
- I am a slave of Christ and I belong to Him, but I do not believe in the Bible.

- I am a slave of Christ and I belong to Him, but I do not believe in all this stuff with Jesus as the Son of God.

Can you see what deceit many people are living in? So many call themselves Christians but are neither disciples nor slaves of Christ. They are still their own masters and live as they wish. One day, many will perish because salvation is found only in Jesus as Lord.

Many people think everything is all right even though it is not. Many believe they are Christians and, therefore, on their way to heaven, but they have actually never made Jesus their Lord, so they are living in deceit.

Next time you use or hear the word "Christian," think about this:

The word "Christian" was not used at the beginning of the first church, nor Jesus did ever use it. It did not exist at all when Jesus lived here on the earth. It can be found only three times in the whole Bible and is first mentioned eleven years after the starting of the new church. It was something they gave as a sort of nickname to the disciples of Jesus, the ones who devoted their whole lives to following Jesus as Lord and Master, which should be the same today.

To be a Christian means, therefore, to be a disciple of Jesus, or in other words, His apprentice or follower; one who abides by His words and does what He says.

The word "disciple" can be found more than 200 times in the New Testament, which shows clearly that it is more important than the word "Christian."

It is not about calling yourself a Christian or a disciple but laying your life down for Him and confessing Him as Lord. It means that you become His slave, which the word "doulos" refers to. This word is used 125 times in the original text.

CHAPTER SEVEN

Not In Our Own Way

Ifyou ask average people if they are Christians, most of them will say yes. If you ask if they are disciples of Jesus, the majority will certainly look at you surprised and say: "A disciple? What are you talking about?" The reason is a wide misunderstanding of the word "Christian." A big problem today is that many people think it is all right to make your own definition of what it means to be a Christian. Therefore, when you ask someone if they are a Christian, you will often get the answer: "Yes, I am," quickly followed by, "but in my own way."

If you ask further if they think they will go to heaven when they die, they will say, "Yes, I think so. I am a good person." This is what I have experienced many times when I have been talking to people about God and eternal life. Unfortunately, neither homemade definitions of faith nor living an exemplary life not based on the Bible gain one access to heaven.

First of all, nobody will ever get to heaven based on their own deeds. If that was a possibility, then there would have been no reason for Christ to die for us. Deeds cannot possibly save anyone because, as the Bible says, everybody has sinned. (We will look at this later.) That is why being "a Christian in your own way" is completely excluded as a possibility.

Try to imagine that one day you are stopped in traffic by a man who claims to be a policeman and wants to give you a fine of $100 for

39

an offence you do not really understand. You ask him if you can see his police badge because it all seems a little strange. He answers that he does not have a police badge. Then you ask him again if he really is a policeman, to which he answers, "Yes, I am a policeman, but in my own way." You quickly learn that he has never had any police education nor has he done anything that is required to become a policeman. His explanation: "It seemed to be too hard, so I decided to become a policeman in my own way." Would you pay him the $100? Of course not. He is not a real policeman, but a cheat. He is actually a criminal because it is illegal to claim to be a policeman when you are not one.

The truth is that we all know you cannot be a policeman in your own way. It is simply impossible. Being a policeman implies that you have special education, you know the law, and you work under the authorities. In the same way, it is completely impossible to be a Christian in your own way. Being a Christian implies that you are a disciple of Jesus Christ, you know the Word of God, and you work under God's authority. The expression, "I am a Christian, but in my own way," is just as ridiculous as the expression, "I am a policeman, but in my own way."

The other place where many people make a mistake is when we believe we can get to heaven by being good people. No person is good enough for heaven. It is not about taking some of our "good" deeds, adding a little bit of Jesus, mixing it together, and creating a way to heaven. Salvation is found only in Him. That is why we can get to heaven only in His way. Many people might consider themselves good in their own eyes, but the truth is that we have all sinned and deserve eternal condemnation in hell.

Take the Ten Commandments from Exodus chapter 20 and see if you have broken at least one of them. If you have broken just one of the commandments one time, you are guilty of them all.

"For whoever keeps the whole law and yet stumbles in one point, he has become guilty of all." (James 2:10 NAS)

Therefore, if you have only once stolen something or lusted after someone other than your spouse, you are guilty and deserve hell. And if you go through the commandments one after another and read what Jesus says about them, you will quickly see that it looks really bad. See, for example, what Jesus says about the commandment, "You shall not kill." Let me ask you if you have ever killed anyone? The answer will surely be no. Try to read, however, what Jesus says about killing:

> *"You have heard that people were told in the past, 'Do not commit murder; anyone who does will be brought to trial.' But now I tell you: if you are angry with your brother you will be brought to trial, if you call your brother 'You good-for-nothing!' you will be brought before the Council, and if you call your brother a worthless fool you will be in danger of going to the fire of hell."* (Matthew 5:21-22 GNT)

The conclusion from what Jesus is saying here is that we are all murderers because we have all done what He is mentioning here. It means that we all deserve to be thrown into the fire of hell.

When we talk about being a good person, our problem is that we again make our own definition of what it means to be "good." On top of all this, we often compare ourselves to that which is wrong. We are measuring ourselves to the wrong "Standard." We are quick to compare ourselves to our neighbors or our friends and then conclude how we line up. It happens when we are checking to see if we are good people and if we are good Christians.

The Bible, however, warns us against this kind of comparison. It says instead that the Bible is the mirror in which we are supposed to see our reflection. It is in the Word that we can see our condition, and nowhere else. Only in this way can we avoid being led astray.

As I said at the beginning, if we compare ourselves to other people, it easily becomes a situation where one blind person leads another one:

> *"Don't worry about them! They are blind leaders of the blind; and when one blind man leads another, both fall into a ditch."* (Matthew 15:14 GNT)

Let us take one more example so that you can see that according to the Bible you are not a good person but are guilty before God when it comes to deeds. The Bible says that no liar has access to heaven. Have you ever lied? You may not think that it is so bad to lie, at least not bad enough to be thrown into hell for all eternity. Try, however, to see here.

If you lie to a 3-year-old boy or girl, what can they do to you? The answer is: nothing. If you then lie to your spouse, what can they do?

The person in question can get angry and do many other things, depending on their character. If you lie to your boss at work, what can they do? You can get fired. What if you lie to the authorities in the court of law? You can get a fine or be thrown into prison. You see that the same lie can have very different consequences, depending on who you lie to.

What we have to understand is that when we lie, we are not just lying to people but also to God. It is Him who has given us life, and when we lie, we actually lie to Him. That is why lying is serious enough to make people go to hell for all eternity. If you believe that you can get to heaven because you are a good person, it is a sign that you do not know God and His Word. It is really a huge deceit that has led many to perdition.

We are all guilty, but we can receive salvation and forgiveness when we make Jesus our Lord and Savior. There is no way in which we can deserve anything from God. It is all about receiving His mercy and forgiveness. Neither you nor I are good people, and if it was up to profit, we would perish. Salvation can be received only due to Jesus Christ and His offering on the cross. It is very important to understand this so that we do not try to earn God's grace, believing that good deeds can save us. The only thing we can do is to say, "Lord, here I am. Save me. Show me Your mercy, and take me as I am."

When we do this, He will receive us, not because of ourselves, but because of Him. God loves us and longs for us. He showed this to us when He forgave us through His son, Jesus Christ.

"For God loved the world so much that he gave his only Son, so that everyone who believes in him may not die but have eternal life. For God did not send his Son into the world to be its judge, but to be its savior." (John 3:16-17 GNT)

CHAPTER EIGHT

MANY "CHRISTIANS," FEW DISCIPLES

W e cannot live as Christians in our own way. Becoming a Christian can only happen in one way: His way. Getting to heaven as a result of our own good deeds is absolutely impossible. Salvation can be found only in Him and in what He has done for us.

Think about those you know who call themselves Christians. Ask yourself if they are actually Christians in their own way, or are they really living as disciples of Jesus, with all the consequences? Then ask yourself if they have really made Jesus their Lord, or are they are still living for themselves and their own way? Some can pass the test, but unfortunately there are so many "Christians" who are not living with Jesus as Lord and Savior. We have many "Christians," but few disciples.

Many people live in self deceit, and as the Bible says, one day they are going to hear Jesus say, "I do not know you. Away from me, you who commit sin". This is an unpleasant thought.

When the Bible says again and again that we should make sure we are not deceived, we have to admit it is extremely relevant. This message undoubtedly seems very radical, but this is because we have gone so far away from the truth. The deception has sneaked in slowly enough for us not to notice how bad it actually is. Today, many Christians are not aware that they do not live according to the Bible and that Jesus is not their Lord. Instead, they compare themselves to people around them and to what their culture says about being a Christian. In this way, many people have assumed that Jesus can be your Savior, but not necessarily your Lord. This possibility is unfortunately excluded from the Bible.

Ask yourself these questions as well:

Am I a disciple of Jesus?

Is He my Lord, or am I still living for myself?

If you realize that you are not a disciple of Jesus, you have to do something about it before it is too late. Afterwards, you have to warn the ones you know who are living in the same deceit. May this book help you reveal this deceit so that many people can make Jesus their Lord and get saved. May the churches begin to preach the Gospel as it is written, and not as our culture says it is.

Our gospel today might create "Christians," but only a few of them are actually disciples and slaves of Jesus.

At the beginning of this book, I mentioned Jesus' warning that one day people will say, "Lord, Lord" to Him, to which He is going to answer, "I have never known you, away from me you who commit sin."

When the Bible says in other places that in the end times love will grow cold and many will fall away from the faith, it is exactly because they listen to wrong teaching.

CHAPTER NINE

TO OBEY JESUS

One of the biggest idols today is materialism, or money. Because of materialism, many people do not have time to serve God. In other words, they choose to spend their life working and earning money, instead of giving themselves to God. The reason is not a lack of time, but a lack of prioritizing. All people have the same amount of time, but they do not all find themselves in the same situations. You cannot have this world and its pleasures and, at the same time, serve God. It is either/or, says Jesus clearly:

"No servant can be the slave of two masters; such a slave will hate one and love the other or will be loyal to one and despise the other. You cannot serve both God and money." (Luke 16:13 GNT)

Again the word *doulos* is used here and is correctly translated as "slave." No slave can serve two masters. It is impossible in itself, so we must choose.

I hope you understand that I am not writing this to condemn anyone. I simply want to point out what is written in the Bible, after which the Holy Spirit must come and convince us. However, I believe this is the reason why so many people today do not see the life we read about in the Bible. We have misunderstood this very significant part of Christianity, namely how you become a Christian and what it means to be a Christian.

When these things line up, you will also experience that God is the same today as He was in the early church. Then you will experience fire, power, and fellowship with Him the same way the first Christians did. The essence is therefore is discovering whether the Word of God is true, whether Christ is really in us, or whether we are deceived.

> *"Put yourselves to the test and judge yourselves, to find out whether you are living in faith. Surely you know that Christ Jesus is in you?— unless you have completely failed."* (2 Corinthians 13:5 GNT)

I am not saying that you should drop whatever you are doing and run into the street in order to try to obey Christ out of pure fear. The purpose is not just to obey, even though it may sound like that, because, if we are obedient out of false motives, it does not bring much profit. It means we are focusing on deeds, doing things to win God's favor or reward, which is wrong. The essence is much greater than deeds. It is whether Christ is living in us and we in Him, abiding in Him and His Word, letting the Holy Spirit show us who we are in Him and how we should live. It comes from the inside as Life and not as dead works, or deeds.

Some people have asked me why I am not simply living for myself and whether it is hard to do what God is saying to me. This does not make sense because nothing could be more wrong. It is not a problem to obey what God is saying to me. When He calls me to do something, I know it is going to be good because He is with me all the time. Therefore, when He tells me, through the Bible or directly, about something I should do, I think, "Yes, great, this is going to be good."

I can give you an example. In January 2009, I fasted for 40 days in connection with the book, and God was working in me about being a disciple. On the 39th day of the fast, something very powerful happened. I was on a walk, praying, when I suddenly experienced God speaking to me very clearly: "Go to Nakskov!" Nakskov is a small town in southern Denmark. I became really excited about it and hurried home to tell my wife, Lené, about it. While I was telling her, my tears were flowing down my face over the strong experience of hearing God speak so clearly.

There is really nothing greater than hearing Him speak. The following day we took the whole family to Nakskov to spend a few days with friends. Those were days when God was really working in us. On Sunday, I preached in a church where I also prayed for someone with a painful knee. After the prayer, he was able to go up and down the stairs without the knee creaking. After the meeting, he was very eager to talk to me. He asked with great excitement, "When was it exactly that God told you to go to Nakskov?" I answered that it was Thursday afternoon. He said, "Wow!" and explained that he had seen our website and on Monday, Tuesday, and Wednesday had prayed to God, "Could you send Torben Søndergaard to Nakskov, so he can pray for me to be healed?"

That was very powerful for him, and for us. He had been asking God for three days to send me to Nakskov, after which God clearly spoke to me to go to Nakskov. That experience really opened our eyes to the power of prayer and how God works. When we came home from Nakskov a few days later, we were aware that something significant had happened in us.

When you experience something so fantastic, you want more of it. You desire to do what Jesus asks of you when you know He is directing your path as you obey Him. Sometimes we cannot see it in the moment, but obeying Him is the greatest thing we can do in this life. He loves us, and we owe Him that. Obedience is not a problem when we are overwhelmed by Him. It does not feel like a sacrifice, but rather like being in love. It does not begin by doing a lot of deeds, but by coming to Him and getting to know Him as He is. It means opening your heart to Him and falling in love with Him. Afterward, we can begin doing what we are supposed to do because then it comes as Life from the inside of us.

If you feel it is about your good deeds, take a pause, lay aside those things, and seek Jesus. Being a Christian means Life in Christ, not deeds or heavy burdens.

CHAPTER TEN

WHAT A FANTASTIC LORD

When we talk about being a "slave" of Jesus Christ, the problem we encounter is the very negative meaning this word has today. If you mention the word "slave," many people think about slavery in the United States until the end of the 19th century, or in southern Europe where millions of Black Africans were sent.

For current generations, slavery is an image of oppression, and that is probably why Bible translators decided to translate the word *doulos* as "servant" instead of "slave." Being a slave does not, however, need to be something negative. It depends on whose slave you are and what your master is like.

If the slave owner is evil, being a slave can be a terribly oppressive experience. If the master is kind and loving, it can actually be fantastic and liberating.

When the slaves in America got their freedom through the Civil War in 1861 through 1865, many of them decided to stay at their masters' homes instead of leaving. They did not consider being a slave in the places they had served to be something grievous or negative. Many of them regarded themselves as free, not as slaves. They loved their masters so much that they wholeheartedly wanted to serve them, and that was why they stayed. They had been treated right and wanted to reciprocate that.

If slaves in those times could have this kind of relationship with their earthly masters, how much more should we have it with Christ? The Bible emphasizes clearly that human beings are basically evil, and only one Person—God—is really good all the time. If man then can enjoy being a slave of a human being who is basically evil, he should much more enjoy being a slave of Christ.

Being a slave of Christ is by no means a terrible life. It is a life where we can bring Him glory by serving Him, where we wholeheartedly want to please Him. We can reciprocate His goodness, although we can never come close to repaying the price He paid for us.

In 1 Corinthians 6, Paul is talking about marriage and fornication. At the end, he uses some strong language.

> *"Flee immorality. Every other sin that a man commits is outside the body, but the immoral man sins against his own body. Or do you not know that your body is a temple of the Holy Spirit who is in you, whom you have from God, and that you are not your own? For you have been bought with a price: therefore glorify God in your body."* (1 Corinthians 6:18-20 NAS)

The truth is that no matter whether we call ourselves Christians, disciples, or slaves, we do not belong to ourselves. We have been bought with a very high price and now belong to someone else, namely Jesus Christ. When He died on the cross, He paid for you and me with His blood, so now He owns us. He is our Lord because that is what ownership means. Our life is surrendered to Him completely voluntarily.

Before reacting to "being owned," let me point out that even before Jesus bought us, we were not free and did not own ourselves. Actually, we have never been free. As the Letter to the Romans emphasizes in many places, we used to be slaves of sin and this world. We used to belong to sin and to the god of this world, namely Satan. That was the life from which we were redeemed.

In John's first letter, he uses the expressions, "children of the devil" and "children of God." The difference between being one or the other can be seen in how one lives and which masterthey are serving. People who have not repented and turned to Christ still live as slaves of sin. They follow the sinful lusts and are called "children of the devil" because they belong to him and serve his agenda, even if they go to church and call themselves Christians. However, when you repent in your heart and receive Jesus as Lord, His blood pays your penalty. You do not belong to sin any longer. On the contrary, you become a slave of Jesus and righteousness. Our affinity will become clear through our lifestyle. Either you are a slave of sin, which leads to death, or of righteousness, which leads to eternal life.

> *"Little children, let no one deceive you. Whoever practices righteousness is righteous, as he is righteous. Whoever makes a practice of sinning is of the devil, for the devil has been sinning from the beginning. The reason the Son of God appeared was to destroy the works of the devil. No one born of God makes a practice of sinning, for God's seed abides in him, and he cannot keep on sinning because he has been born of God. By this it is evident who are the children of God, and who are the children of the devil: whoever does not practice righteousness is not of God, nor is the one who does not love his brother."* (1 John 3:7-10 ESV)

It does not mean that we used to be free and belonged to ourselves, and when we became Christians, we got bound and began to belong to someone else. Nor does it mean that we used to be bound, but when we became Christians, we were redeemed, so now we are free to do whatever we want.

It is true that, as Christians, we have been redeemed from slavery to sin and this world, but not in order to live our own life; we now belong to Him. As Christians, we are free from sin, free to say, "Lord, what is your purpose for me?" We are free to serve Jesus as our Lord and to do His will.

Remember still that our service to Christ comes from within when we become born again. Our rebirth means that serving Him is not a heavy burden. In Him, we receive power to say no to this world and yes to Him.

> *"According as his divine power hath given unto us all things that pertain unto life and godliness, through the knowledge of him that hath called us to glory and virtue ..."* (1 Peter 1:3 KJV)

The question then is not whether we want to be free or to be bound, but to whom we desire to be bound. To whom do we want to belong and obey: sin, which leads to death, or righteousness, which leads to eternal life?

That is why the essence of Christian life is, as we read in 1 Corinthians, that we honor God with our bodies, since now we belong to Him.

In Romans 6, Paul is also talking about being a slave of sin. The word in the original language is still *doulos*.

> "... *knowing this, that our old man was crucified with Him, that the body of sin might be done away with, that we should no longer be slaves of sin. For he who has died has been freed from sin.*" (Romans 6:6-7 NKJV)

> "*And having been set free from sin, you became slaves of righteousness. I speak in human terms because of the weakness of your flesh. For just as you presented your members as slaves of uncleanness, and of lawlessness leading to more lawlessness, so now present your members as slaves of righteousness for holiness. For when you were slaves of sin, you were free in regard to righteousness. What fruit did you have then in the things of which you are now ashamed? For the end of those things is death. But now having been set free from sin, and having become slaves of God, you have your fruit to holiness, and the end, everlasting life. For the wages of sin is death, but the gift of God is eternal life in Christ Jesus our Lord.*" (Romans 6:18-23 NKJV)

Before Jesus saved us, we were slaves to sin. But on the cross, Jesus redeemed us with His blood, so that we no longer yield to sin but to righteousness. That is what happens in salvation and baptism. We are redeemed from slavery to sin and become slaves of Christ instead. This life is completely different from how we lived before.

CHAPTER ELEVEN

BAPTIZED TO BELONG TO CHRIST

To be a Christian means to be a disciple and a slave of Christ. A very important part of becoming a disciple is water baptism. Let's look further at water baptism.

Baptism is the first thing Jesus mentions in the Great Commission, but we have misunderstood its meaning in today's world. Baptism is a transition from one state to another. You are buried with Christ and raised to a new life, a life where you now belong to Christ.

Baptism is really so important that you cannot find a single place in the New Testament where someone starts to believe, but does not get baptized immediately. You can see the same pattern, whether it was in the middle of the night, as with the prison guard and his family in Acts 16, or whether it was the three thousand people who began to believe at the same time, as was the case after Peter's preaching on the day of Pentecost.

The Ethiopian eunuch who heard the Gospel through Philip also got baptized right away. When Philip preached the Gospel to him in Acts chapter 8, what he preached was not written, but we can understand that, in some way, he preached baptism as the introduction to salvation in Christ. It is shown clearly in the eunuch's response to the preaching:

"... See, here is water. What hinders me from being baptized?" (Acts 8:36 NKJV)

Water baptism is a very important part of becoming a disciple. Some might object: "Then what about the thief on the cross? He was not baptized, so did he get saved?" The answer is: No, he did not get baptized, but you have to remember that the New Covenant (The New Testament) was first introduced on the cross. The thief could not be baptized in the name of Jesus because baptism is the image of the death, burial, and resurrection of Jesus. At that time, Jesus was still hanging by his side, alive. Baptism into Jesus had not been introduced at that time. After the cross, however, we see that everybody who came to believe was baptized immediately. Baptism in the New Testament is, therefore, an introduction to life with Christ.

Today, people are baptized "in the name of the Father, the Son, and the Holy Spirit," which is due to a wrong translation in most Bibles. A more correct translation, when it comes to baptism in the Great Commission (Matthew 28:19), is "into" instead of "in," as it says, for example, in the American Standard Version. You do not get baptized "in" the name of the Father, the Son and the Holy Spirit, but "into" the name of the Father, the Son, and the Holy Spirit. In other words, you get baptized "to belong" to the Father, the Son, and the Holy Spirit. In baptism, you are renouncing yourself to belong to someone else. In this case it is God in the Trinity because we get baptized into Him.

Here is Matthew Henry's Commentary* on baptism in Matthew 28:16-20:

> "We are baptized, not into the names, but into the *name*, of Father, Son, and Spirit, which plainly intimates that *these three are one, and their name one.* (...) Our consent to a covenant-relation to God, *the Father, Son, and Holy Ghost.* Baptism is a *sacrament*, that is, it is *an oath; super sacramentum dicere*, is *to say upon oath.* It is an oath of *abjuration*, by which we renounce the world and the flesh, as rivals with God for the throne in our hearts; and an oath of *allegiance*, by which we resign and give up *ourselves* to God, to be *his*, our own selves, our whole selves, *body, soul, and spirit*, to be governed by his will, and made happy in his favour; *we become his men*, so the form of homage in our law runs. Therefore *baptism* is applied to the *person*, as *livery* and *seisin* is given of the premises, because it is the person that is dedicated to God. [1.] It is into the name of *the Father*, believing him to be the *Father of our Lord Jesus*

Christ (for that is principally intended here), by *eternal generation*, and *our* Father, as our Creator, Preserver, and Benefactor, to whom therefore we resign ourselves, as our absolute *owner* and *proprietor*, to actuate us, and dispose of us; as our supreme *rector* and *governor*, to rule us, as free agents, by his law; and as our *chief good*, and *highest end*."

This commentary would be good to read in connection with baptism today. Baptism is something we easily misunderstand, since, in our culture, we do not relate to it in the same way as the Jews. If people understood what baptism really means, many would definitely consider one more time before getting baptized. Then they would know that baptism means renouncing your own will and deciding to belong to someone else, namely Christ. We can see from the Word of God and the pattern in the Acts that baptism is necessary to become a disciple of Jesus Christ.

*http://www.biblegateway.com/resources/matthew-henry/Matt.28.16-Matt.28.20

CHAPTER TWELVE

Baptism In The Holy Spirit

J ust as water baptism is necessary to become a disciple of Jesus, baptism in the Holy Spirit is important for us to be able to live as disciples. It is something that, just as water baptism, has created some controversy in various church circles. The problem that arises over and over again, as I wrote at the beginning of this book, is that we compare ourselves to our church culture and people around us instead of what the Bible says. If you were the only Christian on earth, and had nothing other than the Bible to which you could compare yourself, the question of the baptism in the Holy Spirit would be a very simple and natural part of being a Christian.

When I say that we should compare ourselves to the Bible, I mean that we should read and know the Bible as it is instead of interpreting it through long and complicated theological studies. We should not listen to people who try to deprive Christianity of life and power. If we read the Bible as it is, without our "cultural glasses" and heavy theological explanations, things such as water baptism and baptism in the Holy Spirit will become easy to understand.

Just like with water baptism, there is also a very clear pattern all through the Book of Acts when they talk about baptism in the Holy Spirit. This pattern shows distinctly that, first of all, baptism in the Holy Spirit is important for us to be able to live as disciples of Jesus. Secondly, it is available to all believers and not just to a handful of chosen ones.

Thirdly, getting baptized with the Holy Spirit is visible. Other people are able to see the sign that the Holy Spirit has come upon a person, and you won't be in doubt either that many things happen with you in your baptism in the Holy Spirit. Fourthly, you can see that, in most cases, baptism in the Holy Spirit happens by others who have the Holy Spirit laying hands on you.

We are going to take a look at all this.

There are some Christians today who have misunderstood baptism in the Holy Spirit. They think it is the same as water baptism. Many believe as well that Pentecost in chapter 2 of Acts was the moment when the Christians got saved and received the Holy Spirit for the first time. That is not the case, however. You can read that right after His resurrection, or after the introduction of the new covenant, Jesus paid a visit to His disciples. It says: *"He breathed on them and said to them, 'Receive the Holy Spirit'"* (John 20:22 NAS).

They received the Holy Spirit, or got saved, as we do it today. Still, Jesus said to those who had received the Holy Spirit that they should wait in Jerusalem until they were baptized in the Holy Spirit, although they had already been saved and had the Holy Spirit in them. This is where many people make a mistake, by believing that salvation by the Holy Spirit is the same as getting baptized with Him. This is incorrect, and it is not the pattern we see in the Bible. They are two very distince experiences involved.

Jesus commanded His disciples, those who already had the Holy Spirit in them:

> *"... not to leave Jerusalem, but to wait for what the Father had promised, 'Which,' He said, 'you heard of from Me; for John baptized with water, but you will be baptized with the Holy Spirit not many days from now. ... but you will receive power when the Holy Spirit has come upon you; and you shall be My witnesses both in Jerusalem, and in all Judea and Samaria, and even to the remotest part of the earth.'"* (Acts 1:4-5, 8 NAS)

Baptism in the Holy Spirit is therefore an important part of being a Christian, just like water baptism is necessary to become one. When you talk about becoming a Christian, you can see the same three things coming up: repentance before God, water baptism, and baptism in the

Holy Spirit. Sometimes baptism in water is done first, and people get baptized with the Holy Spirit afterward. In other cases, they first get baptized with the Holy Spirit and then in water.

A few examples:

> *"While Peter was still speaking these words, the Holy Spirit fell upon all those who heard the word. And those of the circumcision who believed were astonished, as many as came with Peter, because the gift of the Holy Spirit had been poured out on the Gentiles also. For they heard them speak with tongues and magnify God. Then Peter answered, 'Can anyone forbid water, that these should not be baptized who have received the Holy Spirit just as we have?' And he commanded them to be baptized in the name of the Lord ..." (Acts 10:44-48 NKJV)*

Here Peter is talking to Cornelius and his family. In these verses, we are reading clearly that they first got baptized in the Holy Spirit and then in water. This shows that water baptism and baptism in the Holy Spirit are two different things.

We also read here, just like in other places in the Bible, that the Holy Spirit descended upon everyone. Baptism in the Holy Spirit is not just for a handful of chosen Christians.

At the beginning of chapter 19 of the Acts, Paul is in Ephesus. There he met some Christians who did not know anything about baptism in the Holy Spirit or water baptism as instituted by Jesus. They had only been baptized in the way John the Baptist practiced it, namely repentance baptism in water.

What did John the Baptist say to the ones baptized by him?

> " *I indeed baptize you with water unto repentance, but He who is coming after me is mightier than I, whose sandals I am not worthy to carry. He will baptize you with the Holy Spirit and fire." (Matthew 3:11 NKJV)*

Later, when Paul pays a visit to Ephesus, we read:

> *"While Apollos was in Corinth, Paul traveled through the interior of the province and arrived in Ephesus. There he found some disciples and asked them, 'Did you receive the Holy Spirit when you became believers?' 'We have not even heard that there is a Holy Spirit,' they*

answered. 'Well, then, what kind of baptism did you receive?' Paul asked. 'The baptism of John,' they answered. Paul said, 'The baptism of John was for those who turned from their sins; and he told the people of Israel to believe in the one who was coming after him—that is, in Jesus.' When they heard this, they were baptized in the name of the Lord Jesus. Paul placed his hands on them, and the Holy Spirit came upon them; they spoke in strange tongues and also proclaimed God's message. They were about twelve men in all." (Acts 19:1-7 GNT)

When you read this report and the answer that Paul got, you could almost think he was evangelizing among Christians today:

"We have not even heard that there is a Holy Spirit." (Acts 19:2 GNT)

The concept of the Holy Spirit and baptism in the Holy Spirit is something that has been suppressed, and this could be one of the reasons why in many places today you cannot see the same life and power we read about all the time in Acts. In this text, we can also see that water baptism into Jesus and baptism with the Holy Spirit are two different things. Here, they first get baptized in water unto Jesus, and afterward in the Holy Spirit, as Paul lays hands on them. Again, we see that they all clearly began to speak in tongues and prophesy, just like it happened with Cornelius and his family.

I have personally prayed for many who got baptized with the Holy Spirit. How can I know that? Just like we read in the Book of Acts, we can see today that people start to speak in tongues, prophesy, or praise God. I can see a significant transformation in their lives later as well.

Many people operate in the Holy Spirit's power immediately. They begin to cast out demons and pray for the sick to be healed. They preach the Gospel with a boldness they had not shown before.

Everything we read about in the Book of Acts is the same today. It is still easy to see when people are baptized with the Holy Spirit, just like it was in the whole Book of Acts, such as this passage in chapter 8:

"Then Peter and John placed their hands on them, and they received the Holy Spirit. Simon saw that the Spirit had been given to the believers when the apostles placed their hands on them ..." (Acts 8:17-18 GNT)

It was easy for Simon to see that the people around him had been baptized with the Holy Spirit, but what did he see? It is not written in this passage that they spoke in tongues or prophesied, but when Simon was able to see the result, we can believe it was so.

When I am addressing speaking in tongues in connection with the baptism in the Holy Spirit, this is something that is available to everyone. It is different from the *gift* of tongues, one of the power gifts shown in 1 Corinthians 12:10, where one gives a message that must be interpreted by someone with the gift of interpretation of tongues, or the one we were reading about in Acts 2, where each one in the crowd heard them speak in his own language.

Many people make a mistake because they do not understand that the Bible clearly describes many forms of speaking in tongues. When they read that not everyone can speak in tongues, they believe it is true for all forms of speaking intongues, including personal tongues, but that is a wrong perspective. We read that all this is valid for those who believe:

> *"And these signs will follow those who believe: In My name they will cast out demons; they will speak with new tongues; they will take up serpents; and if they drink anything deadly, it will by no means hurt them; they will lay hands on the sick, and they will recover."* (Mark 16:17-18 NKJV)

You can also say that these signs follow those who are baptized with the Holy Spirit.

We have to understand that baptism in the Holy Spirit is crucial. Jesus told His disciples not to leave the city before they were baptized with the Holy Spirit and received power from on high. Scriptures indicate that this baptism is available to everyone, and there are always visible signs when people get baptized. Sometimes people get baptized in water first and then with the Holy Spirit. At other times, it is the other way round. Most often, the Holy Spirit is given through laying hands on people. It is the same today as it was then. If you look at the places where there is not enough power or life, you can surely see that the people there have not been baptized in the Holy Spirit. These two things, baptism in the Holy Spirit and power, go together.

I would like to finish with two things connected with the baptism in the Holy Spirit.

First, it is true that in some places, focus on the Holy Spirit is exaggerated and has resulted in wrong worship of the Holy Spirit and signs—an unhealthy worship where there is no place for Jesus. Remember that the Holy Spirit's primary task is to point us to Jesus Christ, and this is what we should be able to see. The exaggeration seen in some places does not mean that the baptism in the Holy Spirit is not necessary in order for us to live as disciples.

Second, some Christians today have been baptized with the Holy Spirit but do not speak in tongues. This is because they have received wrong teaching that has created fear in them. The result is that they do not dare speak in tongues. They already have the Holy Spirit and want to be able to speak in tongues, but they hold it back due to fear. What they need is to start speaking in tongues boldly and to walk in what we read about in the Bible.

Unfortunately, Satan has succeeded in creating confusion around the baptism in the Holy Spirit, just like he has made us believe wrongly that water baptism is unimportant. He knows that if we, as Christians, really get hold of what God has for us, we will have greater victory than ever before.

Both water baptism and baptism in the Holy Spirit are very important in following Jesus.

CHAPTER THIRTEEN

REVELATION AND LIFE

Some years ago, when I had religion classes at school, we were told that Christianity is what you call "a scripture religion." It means that Christianity is based on a scripture, contrary to other smaller religions that are based on traditions. I would not, however, describe it this way. First of all, I do not like to use the word "religion" to describe life with Christ. It is something much more than religion.

Second, I would rather call Christianity "a revelation religion" than "a scripture religion." Of course, Christianity is based on the Bible, but this is something more than a scripture filled with words. It is full of revelation.

> *"Then Jesus said to those Jews who believed Him, "If you abide in My word, you are My disciples indeed. And you shall know the truth, and the truth shall make you free.'"* (John 8:31-32 NKJV)

When Jesus says that, as His disciples, we must abide in the Word and get to know the truth, which will set us free, He is talking about the revealed truth. We can hear the truth and say that now we know it. However, the truth must first become a revelation to us in order to set us free and create life.

This is also valid when the Bible says that we have been redeemed from the slavery of sin. When this is revealed to us, it will create great freedom concerning sin, as well as our relationship with Christ.

Many people who go to church today are still living as slaves to sin. In some cases, the reason is that they are not born again. They have never really made Jesus their Lord and Savior. Another reason is that many people lack a revelation. They have not received a revelation of what Jesus actually did for them on the cross. They have heard about it and understood it with their mind, but it has not yet become a revelation and Life for them.

I have, for example, often heard Christians saying that living as a Christian is hard because there are so many things you must not do and other things you have to do. This is, however, not the way you should feel. As we have mentioned before, Christian Life is something that should naturally flow from the inside. These statements reveal the actual problem, that the person lacks revelation and Life. In some cases, they have not been born again.

I remember so clearly how God saved me. I immediately experienced freedom I had not had before. I had actually not known anything about the Bible until that time, but I felt free to do good things and serve God, which can be hard to explain and hard for others to understand if you have not experienced it yourself. However, those who have experienced it know exactly what I mean. Later in my life with God, I received greater revelation about my freedom in Christ in relation to sin, and then I became even more free.

Due to lack of revelation or not surrendering to Jesus, many people experience, as a rule, that it is difficult to serve God, especially when it comes to sin and living a pure life. This is unfortunately something we see more and more among Christians today. The reason is that we compromise with the Gospel.

We start seeker-friendly churches where the Gospel does not sound as radical as it is. We used to talk about dying to ourselves and this world and laying our life down by the cross, but today we are talking about how to have our best life here and now. Unfortunately, this is the focus in many churches today. We are talking about how we can be happy and succeed here in this life instead of about how we can die to ourselves so that Christ can live through us. We talk about how good and fantastic we are as people and about our potential to be happy, not about how miserable and sinful we are in ourselves, and that this is why we can find life and righteousness only in Christ. When we compromise with the Gospel in this way, it does not bring freedom and salvation but bondage and eventually eternal perdition.

It may not sound this way at the beginning, but true freedom is in Christ and not in compromising and allowing in a little bit of the world. That is why you have nothing to win by compromising with the Gospel.

Jesus paid a high price to redeem us all in order to have a purified and obedient people who serve Him with their whole hearts. This is possible because He has redeemed us for that purpose.

Getting saved or starting to believe is something supernatural, which we must never forget. It is not just a question of beginning to believe in God and going to church, but of getting born again of God. This does not just happen through a prayer we repeat after the pastor or through raising our hand. Neither does it happen when we get a little water sprinkled on our head or become a member of a church. It happens when we see our sin, lay down our life for Christ, and make Him our Lord and Savior.

You have to be born again as Jesus says in John chapter three. When this happens, you are redeemed, and then you will experience that something new has started. You are hungry for the Word, you abide by it and experience how the Holy Spirit keeps on revealing this for you so you become even more free.

Recently, a girl said to me that she would like to have the same faith in God that I had. She thought, however, it would seem fake if she just decided to believe when she was not completely ready to give her life. I said to her that faith is not what she thought it was. Faith is not something human, as we tend to perceive it. This is not something we just start to do with our mind of reason. Faith is supernatural! It is something God puts in us when we turn to Him.

What can possibly make people choose to stay inside a burning house and die rather than deny the faith and be allowed to get out of the flames? This is what happens with Christians today in the most persecuted areas of the world. Thousands of Christians die for their faith every year. This kind of faith is much more than you can imagine with your mind or get by going to church.

Not so long ago, we as a family faced big challenges that really required God's intervention. Those challenges made me feel pressed like never before, and I sought God like never before. There was a period when I prayed six to eight hours every day because I was not able to do anything else. One Thursday evening when I was walking and praying, I experienced a violent demonic struggle, so I prayed even more and quoted the Word of God to make that disappear. I had experienced this once before in the same way until the breakthrough came.

The following day in the evening, after that violent struggle, I suddenly felt great supernatural faith coming upon me. I suddenly became filled up with faith as never before. It seemed tangible, and I felt I could resurrect the dead if there were any. It is hard to explain, but I could feel the faith, and I knew that the answer to our prayers would come. I knew that nothing was impossible for God.

I also received great peace as if I had already received the answer to the prayer for our situation. It was strange to sleep that night. I woke up every hour, filled up with that faith. Although the circumstances still looked hopeless in the natural and I knew I would have to see a miracle before Monday morning, I was sure that God was in control.

On Saturday morning, I said to my wife, Lene, that the solution would come that day. I knew it, not because I saw it, but because I had faith from God. Some hours after that, I received a phone call from a friend from Wales. That same night, he had been awakened by God at four o'clock and received a word for me. That word changed everything, and we could see that God intervened in the last moment.

This is just an example of how real faith can be.

Many people go to church every Sunday without having stable faith. They are still in doubt as to whether everything about God is true and whether they are saved.

If we compromise with the clarity and sharpness of the Gospel, we will not experience true faith and the Life that the Bible talks about. We will not experience the life of the first Christians in Acts, where they could not stop talking about everything they had seen and heard. That was a result of the Life that sizzled out from within. They were not filled with this Life, but the Life of the Holy Spirit.

"Whoever believes in me should drink. As the scripture says, 'Streams of life-giving water will pour out from his side.' " (John 7:38 GNT)

We might get a lot of people to come to our churches by compromising the sharpness of the Gospel, and this is unfortunately what we see more and more often today. But freedom and Life can be found only in making Jesus our Lord and abiding in Him and His Word. True freedom and Life come from the revelation that we can experience through getting filled with Him and His Holy Spirit. We must never forget this.

CHAPTER FOURTEEN

HONOR GOD:
YOUR SPIRITUAL SERVICE

We will now take a closer look at another expression that is misunderstood today, and that is the word "service." When we hear this expression, it can stimulate various thoughts and feelings. Whether we go to an evangelical church or a more traditional one—it is common to both groups—a "service" is something that takes place in a building called a church and consists of songs and teaching. Most Christians treat church services as something very holy. That is why, when you go to a service on Sunday, many Christians put on smart clothes and behave in a particularly nice and respectful way.

This is clearly, more or less, how most of us imagine a church service today. If we study the Bible and church history, however, we discover something totally different. The first church building as we know it was not built until the fourth century. During the first 300 years of church history, meetings took place in various homes, not in a designated "holy" church building.

It is actually not *where* Christians gather that makes a big difference. What matters is our understanding of the church service. Many people imagine a service as something that is held in a particular place, at a particular time, with a particular person (a priest or a pastor) who does particular things. But this is very distant from what God had planned.

We say today that we "go to a service" or "are in church," but the truth is that we ourselves are church, and the service is our life. The church does not consist of dead stones, as all the other buildings. What Jesus wants is to have a church consisting of living stones, where He Himself is the Cornerstone.

> *"Come as living stones, and let yourselves be used in building the spiritual temple, where you will serve as holy priests to offer spiritual and acceptable sacrifices to God through Jesus Christ."* (1 Peter 2:5 GNT)

We are all living stones used in building the spiritual temple, as it says here. We are holy priests who bring spiritual sacrifices to God through our relationship with Jesus Christ. We are a temple for the Holy Spirit. The only building God needs today is you and me. If we understand this, it will create true fear of God and respect for Him. Consider that you as a Christian are a temple for God's Holy Spirit. Consider that God lives in you through His Spirit.

> *"Or do you not know that your body is a temple of the Holy Spirit who is in you, whom you have from God, and that you are not your own? For you have been bought with a price: therefore glorify God in your body."* (1 Corinthians 6:19-20 NAS)

We do not own ourselves anymore. God has bought us with the blood of Jesus so that the Holy Spirit could move in and make our bodies into His holy temple. He owns us, so we have to honor Him with our life. This is our spiritual service.

> *"So then, my friends, because of God's great mercy to us I appeal to you: Offer yourselves as a living sacrifice to God, dedicated to his service and pleasing to him. This is the true worship that you should offer. Do not conform yourselves to the standards of this world, but let God transform you inwardly by a complete change of your mind. Then you will be able to know the will of God—what is good and is pleasing to him and is perfect."* (Romans 12:1-2 GNT)

Bringing our bodies as a holy offering is our spiritual service. We are to be holy, just like God is holy. Holiness is our goal, although this is something not spoken about a lot in the churches nowadays.

Service is not really something you go to in a building or at specific times. It is, of course, good that we meet together, and we should continue doing this, but the real spiritual service is to bring yourself as a holy offering to God. When we gather at services, the purpose is not to hear the preaching, but to bring ourselves to God. It is not just something we have to do on Sunday morning. It is also valid on Monday, Tuesday, Wednesday, and the rest of the week.

"Rid yourselves, then, of all evil; no more lying or hypocrisy or jealousy or insulting language. Be like newborn babies, always thirsty for the pure spiritual milk, so that by drinking it you may grow up and be saved. As the scripture says, "You have found out for yourselves how kind the Lord is." Come to the Lord, the living stone rejected by people as worthless but chosen by God as valuable. Come as living stones, and let yourselves be used in building the spiritual temple, where you will serve as holy priests to offer spiritual and acceptable sacrifices to God through Jesus Christ. For the scripture says, "I chose a valuable stone, which I am placing as the cornerstone in Zion; and whoever believes in him will never be disappointed." (1 Peter 2:1-6 GNT)

Christians are those who serve God by bringing themselves as holy offerings to God. This is their spiritual service.

"We have been bought for a high price," says Paul in 1 Corinthians. We have to admit that he is right. God paid an amazingly high price for us, the life of His Son Jesus Christ, on the cross. The price could not be any higher. We can at least honor God with our life because we belong to Him. Paul understood this and really worked hard to please Jesus.

"TMore than anything else, however, we want to please him, whether in our home here or there." (2 Corinthians 5:9 GNT)

That was the goal in his life. He understood that he no longer belonged to himself, but to Christ. He was overwhelmed by Christ in such a fantastic way that he wished others would also experience that.

The way we honor God is by bringing ourselves to Him. It means that we obey our Lord Jesus Christ because, by honoring Jesus, we honor God:

"Nor does the Father himself judge anyone. He has given his Son the full right to judge, so that all will honor the Son in the same way as they honor the Father. Whoever does not honor the Son does not

honor the Father who sent him." (John 5:22-23 GNT)

It is not enough that we belong to Christ and honor him, but He should also be our life. When we are seized by Him, everything else around fades. Then every price will be worth paying, even if it is blood, sweat, and tears, which is quite certain because nobody enters life without going through tribulation.

Unfortunately, very few people really seize Christ. For them, Paul's speech will be empty words or something that seems too radical.

> *"For to me, to live is Christ, and to die is gain. But if I live on in the flesh, this will mean fruit from my labor; yet what I shall choose I cannot tell. For I am hard pressed between the two, having a desire to depart and be with Christ, which is far better. Nevertheless to remain in the flesh is more needful for you. And being confident of this, I know that I shall remain and continue with you all for your progress and joy of faith, that your rejoicing for me may be more abundant in Jesus Christ by my coming to you again."* (Philippians 1:21-26 NKJV)

Paul says that death is nothing but gain and that he wants to leave this life to be together with Christ. The only thing that keeps him on earth is consideration for others so that they can seize Christ, too.

Many people today will say the opposite of what Paul is saying here. "Jesus, you must not come now because I am enjoying life on earth so much. Jesus, you must not come because I first want to get married, have children, travel, etc."

Many Christians do not want Him to come because, to them, life means living on earth, and there is so much they want to achieve here. On the contrary, Paul wanted to come home to Jesus. Staying here was good, but not because he wanted time to achieve lots of things for himself. The only thing that kept him here was to bear fruit in the lives of others, so that they could also seize Christ, just as he had done.

Paul was dead to this world. His life was Christ. His focus was Christ. His desire was to honor Christ with his life, whatever was going to happen to him.

> *"For I know that this will turn out for my deliverance through your prayer and the supply of the Spirit of Jesus Christ, according to my*

earnest expectation and hope that in nothing I shall be ashamed, but with all boldness, as always, so now also Christ will be magnified in my body, whether by life or by death. For to me, to live is Christ, and to die is gain." (Philippians 1:19-21 NKJV)

The goal of true Christianity is that everyone is seized by Christ and that we all bring our bodies as living and holy offering to Him as our spiritual service. That is why there is absolutely nothing negative about being a slave of Christ. It is rather an honor when a man like Paul is seized by Him. Even if it costs us everything, it would not matter because we are already crucified with Him and do no longer live for ourselves. For we who are seized by Christ, death will be a promotion because, then, we will no longer be separated from Him as we are here on earth. Then we will know him fully, and this is something we cannot achieve in this life.

May this not just be theory for us, something that only Paul practiced. May it become something we all grasp.

CHAPTER FIFTEEN

LET NOT MY WILL BUT YOURS BE DONE

This whole speech about being a slave, honoring God with our bodies, and being seized by Christ may sound strange to many people today. Some will think this is too radical, and others might even be scared away from God. But why should we worry about that? It is God who saves people, and if something is true, it should not be hidden but revealed to as many people as possible. It is important to learn that we cannot please everyone because, as Christ's slaves, we cannot serve people and do everything they expect of us. Paul says it so clearly:

"For do I now persuade men, or God? Or do I seek to please men? For if I still pleased men, I would not be a bondservant of Christ. But I make known to you, brethren, that the gospel which was preached by me is not according to man. For I neither received it from man, nor was I taught it, but it came through the revelation of Jesus Christ. " (Galatians 1:10-12 NKJV)

The Gospel we preach is not from humans but Christ's work. We cannot be His slaves and, at the same time, serve our own wishes and needs. It is not the master's task to ask his slave what he wants to achieve in life and then do everything he can so that the slave can succeed. No, it is the slave's task to say: Lord, what do you want from me?

It is very radical to come up with these statements, especially in our western culture, where almost everything is concerned with us and our needs. According to modern Christianity, it is God who is supposed to serve us so we can succeed, and not vice versa: "Give your life to Him, and He will grant all your wishes. He can help you succeed in your life."

The truth is, however, that this is not about you and me, but Someone much bigger, namely Christ. Have you ever thought about what God received from the service last Sunday, instead of talking about what you got out of it? After the service we should ask, "God, was it a good meeting? I hope You liked our worship of You and our offering because we were here for Your sake."

God is not a machine that is supposed to grant our wishes. It is not the master who serves the slave, but the slave who serves the master. That is what it means to "make Jesus our Lord." We put our own needs aside in order to serve Him.

Try to read these radical words of the Lord Jesus yourself. They are seldom read out loud because they contradict what Christianity has become today:

> "Suppose one of you has a servant [slave] who is plowing or looking after the sheep. When he comes in from the field, do you tell him to hurry along and eat his meal? Of course not! Instead, you say to him, 'Get my supper ready, then put on your apron and wait on me while I eat and drink; after that you may have your meal.' The servant [slave] does not deserve thanks for obeying orders, does he? It is the same with you; when you have done all you have been told to do, say, 'We are ordinary servants [slaves]; we have only done our duty.'"
> (Luke 17:7-10 GNT)

Do you think Jesus could say this to His disciples? It is radical, but that is what it is about. A slave's focus is only on one thing: serving his master. Our job is to serve Jesus Christ. It is not a matter of our will being done, but His.

"Lord, what do you want from me?" This is the natural life for those who have been seized by Him. It is not a heavy burden. His will becomes ours when we are one with Him.

The greatest thing we can experience after this life is to hear the well-known words from Matthew 25 from the mouth of Jesus:

'"... Well done, good and faithful servant [slave]*; you were faithful over a few things, I will make you ruler over many things. Enter into the joy of your lord."* (Matthew 25:21 NKJV)

We can experience this joy now when we serve Him. I have experienced this many times when God has called me to do something for Him. At the beginning, I often went through enormous opposition and trials, but afterwards there comes great satisfaction and joy. At first, it is hard to obey, but I have seen many times how He thanked me for my obedience. This is one of the wildest and most beautiful things. It is really fantastic.

I remember that some time ago God said I should write an article for a Christian magazine concerning something that happened in Lakeland, Florida. A lot of Christians in Europe were excited about some meetings there and took a trip to that place. God showed me, however, that the whole thing was not from Him and that He wanted me to take a public stand and warn people against it, which was not easy because, at that time, they had heard almost exclusively good things about it.

I still wrote the article God asked me for, and it caused a lot of trouble, of course. Some of the people I knew called me and said that I could just end my ministry now and that I was opposing God, etc.

A week after my article, there were a lot of positive articles about that place and lots of negative feedback about me and what I had written. When I read that, I went for a walk and prayed. There, I experienced immediately how God spoke to me again and said, "Good, my son. You have been obedient," and I became filled with joy and thought about the verse talking about the first disciples who had also experienced opposition:

"As the apostles left the Council, they were happy, because God had considered them worthy to suffer disgrace for the sake of Jesus." (Acts 5:41 GNT)

When you are obedient and God is with you, people can say whatever they want because we obey God and not them.

Shortly after my article, everything in Lakeland fell apart, and it became visible that what I said was really correct. Obedience to Him, however, causes opposition, even from the church, which is always the hardest.

The experience of how He rejoices over your offering is much bigger than the offering you could bring. The words: "Well done, good and faithful servant" are something we can experience many times in our life and, hopefully, in the day when it really matters. It is my wish, and it should be the wish of all Christians, that one day we will all hear Him say, *"Well done, good and faithful servant."*

James, the author of James' letter, was an important leader in the church in Jerusalem and a physical brother to Jesus. Nevertheless, even though he had something to be proud of, he starts his letter by explaining that he is a slave of Christ.

"From James, a servant [slave] *of God and of the Lord Jesus Christ ..."* (James 1:1 GNT)

He is not saying, "I am a leader in Jerusalem and a brother of the Lord Jesus Christ." No, he knew who he was and what it was about. Later in his letter he says something we can learn a lot from:

"Now listen to me, you that say, 'Today or tomorrow we will travel to a certain city, where we will stay a year and go into business and make a lot of money.' You don't even know what your life tomorrow will be! You are like a puff of smoke, which appears for a moment and then disappears. What you should say is this: 'If the Lord is willing, we will live and do this or that.'" (James 4:13-16 GNT)

These are great words. We have so many plans for ourselves and for our lives, but we forget about one thing—hearing what our Lord wants us to do.

Jesus said that we should pray like this:

"Your kingdom come, Your will be done on earth as it is in heaven." (Matthew 6:10 NKJV)

These are not just some empty words that Jesus is giving us in the Lord's Prayer. No, it should be our prayer and goal in life that His will is done. This is what it means to make Jesus your Lord.

CHAPTER SIXTEEN

THE PRICE OF BEING A CHRISTIAN

We have looked at the different aspects of becoming and being a real Christian. Now it is time to read Jesus' own words about what it costs to follow Him. As we read this, remember that this is the Lord Jesus Christ Himself who talks about the price of following Him. It is also valid for us today, whether we call ourselves Christians, disciples, slaves, or anything else that comes to mind. This is not about what we call ourselves, but about whether we accept the calling Jesus is giving us—a call to follow Him, a call to make Him our Lord and Savior.

Let us take a closer look at what Jesus teaches, but, first, I want to ask you a question. If Jesus says one thing about what it means to be a Christian, and another person says something different, which of these two shall we believe? Who has the truth about being a Christian? The answer is, of course, Jesus.

Unfortunately, we do not always think this way nowadays. Today, we are quick to quote many others, even though they say something else than what Jesus says. If we want to build our life on the Rock, we cannot always build on our culture. We cannot even build on what great Christian writers are saying today if it is not the same as the Lord Jesus says Himself.

If we are supposed to build on the Rock and build something that lasts eternally, we have to build on the words of Jesus in the Bible and not on everything else. Try to remember this when you read the next Bible passages. Remember that what you are going to read is true, although it is very different from what others are telling you today.

In the following Bible passages I have decided to replace the word "disciple" with the word "Christian." The reason is that, even though we have taken a look at these words, it still lies deep in us that "a Christian" and "a disciple" are not the same.

> *"And he said to them all, 'If you want to come with me* [to be Christians], *you must forget yourself, take up your cross every day, and follow me. For if you want to save your own life, you will lose it, but if you lose your life for my sake, you will save it. Will you gain anything if you win the whole world but are yourself lost or defeated? Of course not! If you are ashamed of me and of my teaching, then the Son of Man will be ashamed of you when he comes in his glory and in the glory of the Father and of the holy angels. I assure you that there are some here who will not die until they have seen the Kingdom of God.'"* (Luke 9:23-27 GNT) (bracketed words added)

Jesus is clearly radical when He talks about the price of being a Christian, and it is not only in this context:

> *"No pupil is greater than his teacher; no slave is greater than his master. So a pupil should be satisfied to become like his teacher, and a slave like his master. If the head of the family is called Beelzebul, the members of the family will be called even worse names! So do not be afraid of people. Whatever is now covered up will be uncovered, and every secret will be made known. What I am telling you in the dark you must repeat in broad daylight, and what you have heard in private you must announce from the housetops. Do not be afraid of those who kill the body but cannot kill the soul; rather be afraid of God, who can destroy both body and soul in hell. For only a penny you can buy two sparrows, yet not one sparrow falls to the ground without your Father's consent. As for you, even the hairs of your head have all been counted. So do not be afraid; you are worth much more than many sparrows! Those who declare publicly that they belong to me, I will do the same for them before my Father in heaven. But those who reject me publicly, I will reject before my Father in heaven. Do not think that I have come to bring peace to the world. No, I did not come to bring peace, but a sword. I came to set sons against their*

fathers, daughters against their mothers, daughters- in-law against their mothers-in-law; your worst enemies will be the members of your own family. Those who love their father or mother more than me are not fit to be Christians; those who love their son or daughter more than me are not fit to be Christians. Those who do not take up their cross and follow in my steps are not fit to be my disciples. Those who try to gain their own life will lose it; but those who lose their life for my sake will gain it." (Matthew 10:24-39 GNT)

Now from Luke, chapter 14:

"Once when large crowds of people were going along with Jesus, he turned and said to them, 'Those who come to me cannot be Christians *unless they love me more than they love father and mother, wife and children, brothers and sisters, and themselves as well. Those who do not carry their own cross and come after me cannot be* Christians. *If one of you is planning to build a tower, you sit down first and figure out what it will cost, to see if you have enough money to finish the job. If you don't, you will not be able to finish the tower after laying the foundation; and all who see what happened will make fun of you. "You began to build but can't finish the job!" they will say. If a king goes out with ten thousand men to fight another king who comes against him with twenty thousand men, he will sit down first and decide if he is strong enough to face that other king. If he isn't, he will send messengers to meet the other king to ask for terms of peace while he is still a long way off. In the same way,' concluded Jesus, 'none of you can be a* Christian *unless you give up everything you have."* (Luke 14:25-33 GNT) ("my disciples" replaced with "Christian" in this text for greater understanding)

Wow! What strong words Jesus is using here. Unfortunately, His message is very different from what we are hearing in many places. Today, salvation is almost equal to believing that Jesus has once lived. You may hear things like: "When we do that, we are Christians." In some places, however, this is not enough; there, you also have to pray a prayer that you repeat after someone else, and then you are surely saved. You may also hear: "If you do not follow the Bible fully, you are still a Christian, but just a lukewarm Christian," or a weak Christian, or whatever else you want to call it. One thing is certain, they tell you,

"You will get to heaven when you die because this is what the Bible says." Does it? Is this what the Bible really says?

Is Jesus implying here in Luke 14 that it is all right to love others more than Him? Is the Bible implying that it is all right to live in conscious sin?

Does the Bible say that it is all right to be a lukewarm Christian, and that the lukewarm ones get to heaven?

Try to pay attention to the last words Jesus said here:

"In the same way ... none of you can be a Christian *unless you give up everything you have."* (Luke 14:33 GNT) ("my disciples" replaced with "Christian" in this text for greater understanding)

According to Jesus, we cannot be Christians if we are not willing to pay the price, even if it is everything we own. That is what Jesus said then, and that is what He is saying today. When did we last hear it preached in our churches? The answer might be: Never!

You must be thinking, just like me, that this is radical, but this is true. The reason why we think this is radical, or maybe even too radical, is probably because we have gone so far away from real Christianity. If we read through all the four gospels, we will clearly see that this is what Jesus said: it costs everything to follow Him.

If we want to get saved, we have to make Jesus our Lord and become His slaves. Our own wishes, needs, and dreams cannot be of much use. It is our Lord's will that matters because He has bought us.

CHAPTER SEVENTEEN

PERSECUTIONS AND TRIBULATIONS

One of the things Jesus often talked about was that we, as Christians, should expect persecutions and tribulations. He says even more often that following Him can cost us our life. Europeans and others in free countries can have a big problem understanding the severity of these warnings because of our religious freedom, but this is a reality for thousands of Christians all over the world. If we experienced the same opposition and persecution that our brothers and sisters do in those countries, our European Christianity would look very different.

First of all, it would mean that we could clearly see those who are real Christians and those who just call themselves Christians. Many of the false Christians, i.e., those who still live for themselves, would stop coming to church. They would deny their faith the day it cost them a price they were never willing to pay. I imagine that many churches would become very small in just a few days.

It would also mean that the remaining ones would be those who had really made Jesus their Lord and were willing to pay whatever the cost to follow Him. The opposition would make them seek God as never before, which would bring real growth and maturity. This pattern has been seen throughout history, and I believe it would also happen in Europe, North America, South America, Africa, Asia, everywhere.

It almost sounds as though I want the persecution of churches to come. The truth is that we may need persecution so as not to fall asleep. At the same time, it would reveal the false teachers and the false gospel that is being preached in many places.

In the parable of the sower, Jesus said that it is tribulation and persecution that revealed what was sown on stony ground and what was sown on good ground:

> "But he who received the seed on stony places, this is he who hears the word and immediately receives it with joy; yet he has no root in himself, but endures only for a while. For when tribulation or persecution arises because of the word, immediately he stumbles. Now he who received seed among the thorns is he who hears the word, and the cares of this world and the deceitfulness of riches choke the word, and he becomes unfruitful." (Matthew 13:20-22 NKJV)

It is very hard to see who is sincere and who is not. It is hard to distinguish between those who want to pay the price and those who want to be entertained. Again, it is hard for us because we let ourselves be cheated by numbers and outer things, and lose focus on true devotion and on what lasts eternally.

Let me explain what I mean by this. Since we are not experiencing persecution and tribulation today, it looks like it does not cost so much to become a Christian. That is why we can easily compromise the Gospel without seeing how dangerous it is. Today, we seem to achieve greater growth by compromising the radical message Jesus brought and preaching a human-centered gospel. If you look at the big churches in the West, this is unfortunately a frequent reason; they preach a gospel that talks more about success and happiness than about laying down your life and making Jesus your Lord.

This cheap gospel will never be received in the countries where it costs to be a Christian. Many of our Sunday sermons would be immediately ignored if they were preached to people in heavily persecuted countries.

Just try to imagine messages such as: "Give your life to God, and He will help you to be happy," or "God has a wonderful plan for your life, so just come to Him now." How do you think these messages would be received if one had just seen their family tortured and killed because they had given their lives to Jesus?

The truth is that much of what is preached in the West today would be useless if we had to face persecution. We would then be forced to go back to the Bible and the true Gospel, where it costs everything to follow Jesus. This is where we have to go through many tribulations in order to start the real life, a life with God without any pain, sin, or sickness. Nowadays, we are focusing so much on this life and so little on the life that will come. This would change if the present life became difficult due to tribulations and persecution.

We cannot let ourselves be cheated. We have to preach what the Bible says, even if it does not seem to work. If we start to preach the Gospel today as Jesus did, it will require the Holy Spirit to come and draw people to repentance. Then salvation will be something that God does in a sovereign way, just like in the first church.

This is not the case with the other gospel, where we compromise. We make it sound so appealing to become a Christian that one would have to be stupid not to receive it, but this different gospel does not make a difference and does not bring the Life the Bible talks about. People cannot come to God unless He draws them. Salvation is the sovereign work of the Holy Spirit. We read in the Bible how God was adding people, but will He do it if we are not faithful to His Word?

Jesus said this about those who became Christians:

"... none of you can be my disciple [a Christian] *unless you give up everything you have."* (Luke 14:33 GNT) (bracketed words added)

One day, many ministers will get a hard judgment when it turns out that they have led people astray by preaching another gospel. Many are so driven by a wish to have great numbers that they have compromised what they know is true. They have seen it is easier to get people into the church by preaching something other than what Jesus said we should preach.

I have a motto I want to live out, although it is often difficult. Here it is: *I would rather people curse me now and thank me in eternity than to thank me now and curse me in eternity because I did not preach the truth.*

This is a motto that is incredibly hard to follow because we all want to be praised and liked by people. They can curse us now but thank us in eternity because they heard the truth and repented. That is better than thanking us now for our wonderful sermons and then cursing us the day they die when they perish because Jesus was not their Lord.

We must realize that even though we do not see the price of following Jesus as clearly as those in persecuted countries, it is the same price. Although we do not experience the same persecution, it is still the same Gospel and requires the same personal sacrifices.

We might not have to give up our houses, family and other things in the physical sense to become a Christian, but in order to follow Jesus, we have to renounce them in our hearts so that we can do it without hesitation. Remember what Jesus said:

> "... *none of you can be my disciple* [a Christian] *unless you give up everything you have.*" (Luke 14:33 GNT) (bracketed words added)

God looks at the heart and our willingness or lack of it. If we are not willing to do that, God has to make us willing.

I can say personally that the three years before this book was finished were the hardest years of my life as a Christian. They were full of tests in which God allowed everything to be taken away from my family. One of the things we experienced was losing our house, just as Jesus mentioned. It was not funny to go through, but it was necessary to be able to mature and grow closer to Him.

It is through these kinds of struggles and tests that we see what has true value. At the same time, we find that houses and lands and all the other things we think we need in life have no value when compared to Life in Christ. The only thing that has true value is knowing Jesus. It is seizing and serving Him all the days of our life.

CHAPTER EIGHTEEN

FRIENDS OF JESUS AND CHILDREN OF GOD

Before we finish, we will take a look at what it means to be friends of Jesus and children of God. You are going to notice that this is not contrary to what I have been teaching up to now, even though some may understand it this way.

In a conversation with the disciples soon before the end of the life and ministry of Jesus, He calls the disciples His friends for the first time:

"No longer do I call you servants [slaves], *for the servant* [slave] *does not know what his master is doing; but I have called you friends, for all that I have heard from my Father I have made known to you."* (John 15:15 ESV) (bracketed words added for clarity)

Try to pay attention to what He is saying, or rather, not saying. He is not saying they are not His slaves anymore, but that He is not calling them slaves any longer. Another translation says that He no longer treats them as slaves. In order to understand what Jesus is actually saying here, it is necessary to look at the context. Just before that verse, He says:

"Greater love has no one than this, that someone lay down his life for his friends. You are my friends if you do what I command you." (John 15:13-14 ESV)

When we lay down our own life for Him as slaves and call Him our Lord, Jesus comes to us and says that He no longer treats us as slaves, but as friends.

What a great honor to be called a friend of Jesus. It is amazing to think about. Imagine being friends with HIM who created everything, our Lord and God.

Today, many people take this verse from John 15 and make it sound like Jesus is friends with everyone and everything, which is completely wrong. You first become His friend through salvation by laying down your life for Him and doing what He says. You cannot live as a sinner and, at the same time, be friends with Jesus. Friendship with the world is enmity with God.

You might say it is written in the Bible that Jesus was a friend of sinners and point to this verse:

> "When John came, he fasted and drank no wine, and everyone said, 'He has a demon in him!' When the Son of Man came, he ate and drank, and everyone said, 'Look at this man! He is a glutton and wine drinker, a friend of tax collectors and other outcasts!'" (Matthew 11:18-19 GNT)

This is another verse that is often misunderstood. Of course, Jesus used to spend time with sinners in order to call them to repentance, as the Bible says, but you cannot say on the basis of this verse that He was close friends with them. What we read here is what people said about Him. In the same verse, it also says that Jesus was a glutton and a wine drinker, which He was not. Neither was John the Baptist possessed, as they also claimed in these verses.

Therefore, this friendship that Jesus is speaking of is for those who have laid their life down for Him and made Him Lord. Not everyone shares this friendship with Him, but only those who do what He commands. One day, as we have read, He will say to many: "... *I never knew you. Get away from me, you wicked people!*" (Matthew 7:23 GNT)

We do not see Jesus calling people by saying: "Come and become my friends." No, it starts when we turn away from this world and make Him Lord. Then we become His friends, and He becomes ours.

Another thing that happens in salvation is that God puts a ring on our finger, and we become His son or daughter, as you can read in the parable about the prodigal son.

Even though we become friends with Jesus or children of God, even though we are really adopted by God and can say "Abba, Father," it is still important that we know who we are and who He is.

Joseph, from the Old Testament, was promoted from a slave to a ruler, but even as a ruler, he was still technically a slave for the pharaoh. The pharaoh could degrade him at any time and send him to the dungeons again. The pharaoh's word was still valid, and Joseph had to obey him, even after his promotion to a noble position.

Although Jesus calls us friends and we get this noble honor of becoming God's son or daughter in Christ, we are still like slaves and do not deserve anything else. This means that everything we get is from grace, and we should be thankful for everything.

In other words, it is all about love. You may be surprised by these words right now because not a lot has been written about love in this book. I have been writing a lot about serving Jesus and obeying Him, but serving and obedience should be out of love for Him.

He loves us and showed it by sacrificing His life for us. His love for us, which is beyond any limits, should be the driving force in everything we do.

Jesus said:

"... 'You shall love the Lord your God with all your heart, with all your soul, and with all your mind.' This is the first and great commandment. And the second is like it: 'You shall love your neighbor as yourself.' On these two commandments hang all the Law and the Prophets." (Matthew 22:37-40 NKJV)

It is not hard to love Him when you understand how this is connected. Teaching about being a slave can actually help us to love Him even more when we see that He is really good to us and when we understand that everything we are and get is out of His grace.

We are His slaves, but He treats us like His friends. He loves us more than we will ever understand as long as we are here on earth. As slaves we own nothing and have nothing to say, but still He reaches out and confides things to us.

We were nothing, but due to salvation in Christ, we became children of God. We can call God our Father because that is who He is. Let us, therefore, love Him with all our heart and love our neighbors as ourselves.

King David understood this, too. He did not brag about his success or power as a king. His prayer was like this:

> *"I am your servant, Lord; I serve you just as my mother did. You have saved me from death. I will give you a sacrifice of thanksgiving and offer my prayer to you."* (Psalm 116:16-17 GNT)

Through salvation, we become children of God, and Jesus calls us His friends.

CHAPTER NINETEEN

CONCLUSION

We have taken a look at different aspects of what it means to be a Christian, if I may use the most common term today. Then what is a Christian?

The short answer to what it means to be a Christian is "one who believes in Jesus." The problem is that many people today do not understand all that this implies. They have misunderstood the meaning of faith. Many do not know what Jesus actually teaches. That is why it is impossible for them to believe in Him because believing in Him means to believe both in Him as the only begotten Son of God and in what He teaches. Faith means practising and living by what He says.

In this book, I have tried to put an end to this problem by explaining what it means to believe in Jesus. I have used some other terms that should make it more clear to see what faith in Jesus really is and what it implies.

As you probably see, there are, unfortunately, many who have gone wrong here. One day, many will perish because salvation can be found only in Jesus. It also explains, however, why many churches and Christians lack the Life and the power that the Bible says the first Christians had.

I will now give you a longer and deeper answer to the question, what is a Christian? It is based on the things we have looked at in this book. I could highlight other important aspects that are part of

Christian life, such as church, prayer, care, etc., but I will not deal with them here.

What is a Christian?

A Christian is one who has laid down his life at the cross and made Jesus his Lord and Savior. You show this devotion by being baptized in water in order to belong to Jesus Christ. From that moment, you no longer live for yourself but for the One who died and rose again, Jesus Christ. This is also called repentance.

When you repent before Jesus Christ, you become born again, and the Spirit of God takes residence in you. You are now a new creation, as the Bible calls it, not born of human will but of the Spirit of God. Something supernatural happens within you, and this new birth is the beginning of your Christian walk.

In this new birth, you are also redeemed from the slavery of sin, and that is why now you can bring yourself as a holy, living offering to God. As a "born-again Christian," you can no longer live in conscious sin as before. Your conscience has become new. It is sharp and clean, which makes you notice immediately when you commit sin. It also makes you stop living in sin. You will feel free in relation to sin and strive to live a holy life, in spite of shortcomings and constant struggles against the flesh.

Thus, as a Christian you no longer live for yourself, in conscious sin. You are done with yourself and this world. You do not say anymore: "Let my will be done," but, "Lord, I love You. Let Your will be done in me."

As a born-again Christian, you will also feel natural hunger for the pure milk of the Word, which is the Bible. Just like a healthy baby is hungry for milk, your spirit will cry out for more of God. As a Christian, you remain in the Word (the Bible), and you let the Word guide you and set you free.

> "... If you abide in My Word, you are My disciples indeed. And you shall know the truth, and the truth shall make you free." (John 8:31-32 NKJV)

A Christian is also one who is baptized in the Holy Spirit and experiences His power and life within. Baptism in the Holy Spirit is really important for us to be able to live as Christians. Without it, you are never going to experience the power and revelation that the first disciples had. Through the baptism in the Holy Spirit, as well as personal fellowship with God and His Word, we as Christians find the strength to live the life we read about in the Bible; a life with many challenges and obstacles; a life in the supernatural, where we see how God is close and intervenes daily in many fantastic ways; a life as we read about it in the Book of Acts; a life where you cannot stop talking about everything you have seen and heard.

All these things characterize a Christian life, but in order to receive it, you must absolutely get born again. You should not try to live as a Christian without this new birth because it is impossible. If you try, it will go wrong because, in the new birth, God gives you what is necessary to be able to live with Him. He gives us the Holy Spirit as our Helper and Guide who reveals Christ for us.

Without the new birth, your Christian life will feel like rules and dead deeds, and it will end in perdition. Without Christ, you are going to fail your test. The new birth into God is where it all starts. Unfortunately, many people in the churches today ignore it.

A Christian is also one who really wants to honor God through his life. This happens through honoring the Son and obeying God; through being faithful in what you do; through working as if it was for the Lord (Ephesians 6:7); through laying your life down for your family as if it was for the Lord (Ephesians 5:25); by doing everything as if it was for the Lord.

"And whatever you do in word or deed, do all in the name of the Lord Jesus, giving thanks to God the Father through Him." (Colossians 3:17 NKJV)

"For none of us lives to himself, and no one dies to himself. For if we live, we live to the Lord; and if we die, we die to the Lord. Therefore, whether we live or die, we are the Lord's." (Romans 14:7-8 NKJV)

A Christian lives and breathes for his Lord, Jesus Christ.

In other words, a Christian is a person who loves God with all his heart, all his soul, and all his mind, and he loves his neighbor as himself (Matthew 22:37-40).

As you have read, the Christian life starts with the new birth, but it does not end there because, after the new birth and the baptism in the Holy Spirit, you have to learn to walk and live with God. This walk is to a large extent based on fellowship with God and being a disciple of people who go before us, others who live the life you read about in the Bible.

Discipleship does not only happen through teaching at meetings. It happens mainly through sharing life. It happens through making mistakes and learning from them. It happens through correction and challenges to take responsibility and new steps. It happens through practical things, such as learning to evangelize, learning to pray, fast, and study the Bible, something that is unfortunately emphasized too little today.

Jesus uses this description of being a Christian and belonging to Him:

> *"My sheep hear My voice, and I know them, and they follow Me. And I give them eternal life, and they shall never perish; neither shall anyone snatch them out of My hand."* (John 10:27-28 NKJV)

You can also say that a Christian is one who hears His voice and follows Him. If you do not hear what Jesus says, then you do not follow Him, and you do not belong to him, which implies that you are not a Christian. This is what Jesus Himself says.

My question to you is not whether you are a Christian or whether you are baptized and confirmed. Neither I am not asking whether you believe in Jesus or go to church. My question is: Are you really born again? Are you a disciple of Jesus? Do you hear His voice and follow Him? If not, you must repent today and ask Jesus to save you.

Without His salvation you will perish in hell for eternity. God is a just God, Who will one day judge all people. We are all guilty of sin, and that is why we all need forgiveness. God loves us so much that He gave His only son, Jesus Christ, to die in our place. On the cross, Jesus took the punishment we should have received. He took your sin and my sin on Himself, so that we can be free in Him. We find this forgiveness only in Jesus, by repenting and making him Lord, with everything it implies. I hope you will receive this forgiveness before it is too late.

Seek Him and get to know Him as He is. Read the Bible and let the

Holy Spirit show you how to live. Then find some disciples who can take you into discipleship, some who can go before you, so you can learn and develop. Then you can also begin to make others disciples of Jesus, which is what He commanded us to do.

If you are already living in this, let us stand together and spread the message about being a Christian, disciple, and slave to all those who have not heard it yet. May we understand what it means to be a Christian on a daily basis.

Let us see a New Testament Christianity come back to our land. God is the same today as He was in biblical times.

God bless you.

Torben Søndergaard
A disciple of Jesus Christ

Other Books By
Torben Søndergaard

The Last Reformation
Back to the New Testament Model of Discipleship

Much of what we see expressed in the church today is built on more than just the New Testament. It's built, instead, mostly on the Old Testament, Church culture, and Paganism. It is therefore imperative that we as God's people dare to stop and take a closer look at the Church today and compare it to the first Church we read about in the Bible. If we are to succeed in making disciples of all nations then we must go back to the "template" we find in the Bible.

Let the reformation begin!

Most of us as Christians have inherited a way of being church and being disciples. Torben challenges us to question this by using examples from the Bible and from Church history. This book is challenging and sharp, but we all want to see more people believing in Jesus, disciples trained, and churches growing stronger and multiplying. This is why we believe **The Last Reformation** *is important for our thinking about how we want to be and do church in our times.*

• From the Foreword by Charles Kridiotis and Mattias Nordenberg

This book may be purchased in paperback from USA:
www.TheLaurusCompany.com/store and Amazon.com
Outside the USA: Amazon.ca, .co.uk, .de, .at, .fr, .it, .es
and other retailers around the world.
Also available in electronic reader formats from their respective stores.

Other Books By
Torben Søndergaard

Sound Doctrine

According to the Bible, sound doctrine creates true fear of the Lord. If this fear of the Lord is missing in our churches, as it seems to be, it must be a sign that we do not preach the true Word of God and sound doctrine. Teaching sound doctrine should cause us to see a need to surrender everything to God and to live in the light. There is no darkness, no sin, when we are walking in the light (1 John 1:7).

True godliness and holiness is required to walk with God. In this prophetic word to the Church, Torben brings us back to the Bible where sound doctrine is found, including how to address sin in the church and in the individual.

Has the church been teaching sound doctrine? Has it become soft on sin? Can the church expect its prayers to be answered if there is sin in the camp? Is the church accursed because it has allowed sin to thrive unchallenged? Can a person truly be born again and continue in conscious sin? Have we been teaching a grace that tramples the blood of Jesus? These are serious questions that must be addressed if we expect God to hear our prayers. His word to the church: REPENT!

Other Publications By
Torben Søndergaard

"Christen, Discipel, of Slaff?"
(Dutch language)

"Life as a Christian"

"Complete the Race"

"Deceived?" (Booklet)

"The Twisted Race" (Booklet

These Publications can be found on the author's website at:

www.TheLastReformation.com

About The Author

Torben Søndergaard

Torben Søndergaard lives in Denmark in the city of Herning with his wife, Lene, and their three children.

Torben grew up in a non-Christian family. On April 5, 1995, after attending a church service with a friend, he turned to God and had a strong, personal encounter with Jesus that totally changed his life. Five years later, from a Scripture in the Bible and in a sort of desperation after more of God, Torben started on a 40-day fast that transformed many things in his life. His eyes were more open to God's Word and what the gospel is about. He began to understand how lukewarm and far away from the truth Christians had become. He saw that God had called him to speak His Word without compromise.

Torben has worked as an evangelist and church planter for some years. Today, he is having meetings around Denmark and abroad, where he sees many people getting healed and set free. He is the author of six other books, has been on both radio and TV many times. Apart from that, he is the founder of the websites: OplevJesus.dk, Mission.dk, and the English websites:

TheLastReformation.com and TheLastReformationUSA.com